Get Creative!

with M'Liss Rae Hawley

A Beginner's Guide
to COLOR & DESIGN
for Quilters

C&T PUBLISHING

Text © 2005 M'Liss Rae Hawley

Artwork © 2005 C&T Publishing, Inc.

Publisher: Amy Marson

Editorial Director: Gailen Runge

Acquisitions Editor: Jan Grigsby

Editor: Darra Williamson

Technical Editors: Teresa Stroin and Rene J. Steinpress

Copyeditor/Proofreader: Wordfirm Inc.

Cover Designer: Kristen Yenche

Design Director/Book Designer: Kristen Yenche

Illustrator: Tim Manibusan

Production Assistant: Tim Manibusan

Photography: Sharon Risedorph and Luke Mulks. Author photo by Michael Stadler.

Published by C&T Publishing, Inc., P.O. Box 1456, Lafayette, California 94549

Front cover: The Century of Progress block by the author

Back cover: Interlude in Chartreuse and Red Violet by the author and, Century of Progress by the author and friends

Library of Congress Cataloging-in-Publication Data

Hawley, M'Liss Rae,

      Get creative with M'Liss Rae Hawley : a beginner's guide to
      color & design / M'Liss Rae Hawley.

   p. cm.

  Includes bibliographical references.

  ISBN 1-57120-286-2 (paper trade)

  1. Patchwork--Patterns. 2. Quilting--Patterns. 3. Patchwork quilts.

I. Title. TT835.H3485223 2005

746.46'041--dc22

           2004030541

Printed in China

10 9 8 7 6 5 4 3 2 1

■ Dedication

To my son, Sgt. Alexander Walsh Hawley, United States Marine Corps, and to 3rd platoon, Echo Company, 2nd Battalion, 7th Regiment of the 1st Marine Division, serving in Iraq as I am writing this book. I lovingly dedicate this book to you—for your courage, bravery, and sacrifice—and to all the troops willing to risk all so that others may be free.

Semper Fi

Mom

July 4, 2004
Whidbey Island, Washington

▓ Acknowledgments

This has always been an important part of my books: the individuals and companies with whom I partner share my vision, enthusiasm, and love of quilting. I would most gratefully like to thank them, both personally and professionally, for their contributions to this industry.

C&T Publishing:
    Amy Marson, Jan Grigsby, Darra Williamson, Teresa Stroin, Kris Yenche, and Tim Manibusan

Husqvarna Viking:
    Stan Ingraham, Sue Hausmann, Tony Kowal, Nancy Jewell, and Theresa Robinson

In The Beginning: Sharon Evans Yenter and Jason Yenter

Island Fabrics: Judy Martin

Hoffman Fabrics: Sandy Muckenthaler

Quilters Dream Batting: Kathy Thompson

Robison-Anton Textiles: Bruce Anton and Andreea M. Sparhawk

Primedia: Tina Battock and Beth Hayes

I would like to thank Anastasia Riordan for her friendship, guidance, and moral support on my creative journey.

Thank you also to an exceptional group of quilters who believed in me and in my dream to write this book. (Meet them on page 80.) They worked for over three years, complaining about fabric color, selection, placement, and—of course—deadlines. We laughed, cried, and celebrated together throughout this creative journey.

CONTENTS

Introduction

Throughout my years of teaching and lecturing, I have observed a desire on the part of my students to learn more about color and design. Many quilters enter the world of quilting without an artistic background. Perhaps their only experience with art was in high school, and that—sadly—may have been an unpleasant experience.

I knew someday I would write a book addressing the knowledge my students were seeking. I also knew that the perfect block would appear as a teaching tool when the time was right—and it did!

Over the past century, quilt blocks have been named for places, people, and events. The Century of Progress block draws its name from the Chicago World's Fair of 1933. Many of the blocks entered in the fair's quilt competition were titled Century of Progress, after the event itself. The version featured in this book, credited to Nancy Cabot and first published in *The Chicago Tribune* in 1933 as Block #7, was designated as ideal for beginning quiltmakers.

The 8-inch Century of Progress block includes nine elements—all squares, rectangles, and strips. The simple geometry of its Mondrian style appeals to me. It is the perfect block to use as the focus for the study of color and design. It is easy to enlarge and to rotate. You can change its proportions easily. From a sewing standpoint, there are no points to match and nothing to cause you stress.

As you work your way through the various exercises in this book, I have no doubt you'll agree it is the perfect choice. Because you are free from the distraction of precision piecing, you can focus on color and design. Together we'll explore the color wheel and the variety of color schemes it suggests: achromatic, monochromatic, analogous, and more. We'll also explore the elements of design as they apply to quilting: proportion; composition; and the print, scale, and design orientation of the fabric.

My desire is that you'll use this book to experiment and be playful in your quiltmaking; that you will take this opportunity to learn the rules in order to break them! The object here is growth: What is to be discovered? What is to be learned? Let the simple Century of Progress block be your creative vehicle to an enriching adventure in learning.

So take my hand, and let's go!

Century of Progress *block*

The Language of Color:
Glossary of Color Terms

Here is a collection of common terms as they apply to color, design, fabric, and textiles. Read them over, and refer to them as necessary as you work your way through the various color and design exercises in this book. You may feel this takes you back to your school days—mastering your spelling and vocabulary lists—but trust me: this is a valuable place to begin your journey into the wonderful world of color and design.

Achromatic: Colorless, transparent, having no color. A colorless scheme of black, white, and gray.

A selection of achromatic fabrics

Analogous: Colors that appear side by side on the color wheel, for example, red, red-orange, and orange. Quilts based on this color story work because the three or four colors have an element of color in common with their neighbors.

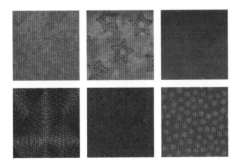

An analogous color scheme

Balance: The comfortable relationship between colors. A good balance of color provides equilibrium in the quilt's design. Complementary parts of the spectrum are represented and work together to form a visually pleasing color scheme.

Black: The darkest of the neutrals and the opposite of white. Black is a very sophisticated color choice for a quilt. It is also the color that represents mourning in the United States.

Chroma: The measurement of a color's purity and intensity, that is, its brightness or dullness as determined by its degree of freedom from white or gray.

Color properties: Qualities by which colors are defined: the hue (the name of the color), the value (measure of lightness or darkness of the color), and the chroma or intensity (the brightness or dullness of the color).

Color wheel: A device designed to illustrate the twelve pure colors—the three primary colors (red, yellow, and blue), the three secondary colors (orange, green, and violet), and the six tertiary or intermediary colors (yellow-orange, red-orange, red-violet, blue-violet, blue-green, and yellow-green)—and the relationships among them. For more on the color wheel, see pages 9–11.

Complementary: Color pairs that appear directly across from each other on the color wheel, for example, red and green, blue and orange, and yellow and purple. Each color is balanced by its opposite (or complementary) color.

Complementary color schemes

Cool colors: The blue, green, and violet members of the color wheel. These colors suggest the peaceful feeling of grass, water, ice, and sky. Cool colors typically recede into the background of a design.

Fabrics in cool colors

Cotton: A natural, cellulosic, seed-hair fiber. This is the fiber most often used in quilting; it is soft, easy to work with, and very forgiving.

Design (verb): To form an idea, an outline, or a draft to project an image, with the end product being a work of art—in this case, a quilt!

Dye: A color, tint, or hue used to color fiber. The source may be natural (*e.g.*, vegetation) or synthetic (*e.g.*, chemical).

Dyeing: The process of applying color to fiber in which the coloring substance becomes an essential part of the fiber. There are many methods to apply dye to fiber, including immersion, discharge, and pigment application.

Fabric: The most general term for describing textiles, embracing cloths, carpets, canings, and rugs.

Fibonacci, Leonardo Pisano: Thirteenth-century mathematician known among designers and artists for his system of proportion based on ratios.

Gray: The result achieved when white and black are mixed.

Gray scale: This tool, which transitions from white through grays to black, is considered fundamental in determining value. The most effective gray scale, which consists of hard-edged blocks of paint (similar to paint chips), passes through at least ten values.

Greige (pronounced "gray") goods: Unfinished or raw fiber, as in fabric that has been woven but not finished or converted by dyeing or printing.

Hand: A term used to describe the tactile properties of fabric; literally, how a fabric "feels" when held in the hand.

Hue: The name of the pure color, without any of the complementary color or any black, white, or gray added, for example, red, blue, yellow, orange, green, and violet.

Intensity: The brightness or purity of a color as compared with gray. A color in its purest state is a completely intense—or saturated—color; it is not diluted.

Intermediary colors: Colors created by mixing a primary and a secondary color, for example, blue-violet (blue and violet), red-orange (red and orange), and yellow-orange (yellow and orange). Also called tertiary colors.

Ives color wheel: An alternative, 24-step color wheel, developed by Herbert Ives, a key figure in the scientific study of photography. This color system, familiar to some quiltmakers, identifies yellow, magenta, and turquoise as the primary colors and orange,

Ives Color Wheel

violet, and green as the secondary colors.

Metallics: Fabrics with shiny metallic threads. These threads include fibers with colorations of copper, gold, silver, platinum, chrome, bronze, steel, and pewter. Metallic threads are also available for embellishment—the possibilities for their use are endless.

Fabrics with metallic accents and a variety of metallic threads for quilting and embellishing

Monochromatic: From the Greek *monos* ("single") and *chroma* ("color"). Describes a color scheme based on a single color in all its various tints, tones, and shades.

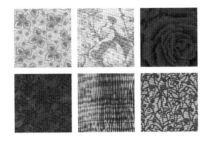

Monochromatic color scheme

Neutral: Free from the mixture of colors; typically includes white, gray, and black. May also include the metallics: gold, silver, platinum, copper, bronze, pewter, and steel. Quilters often select neutral-colored fabrics for use as backgrounds.

Selection of neutrals

Pastels: Whitened-down tints of pure color. These soft, pale colors are associated with spring, Easter, and babies.

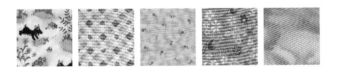

Selection of pastel fabrics

Plain weave: A basic construction in which one warp thread interlaces alternately with one weft thread to form fabric. It is the weave most common in the cotton fabric favored by quilters.

Primary colors: The three pure colors—yellow, blue, and red—that are the basis (by mixing) for all other colors.

Pure color: The color as it appears on the color wheel, for example, without the addition of white, black, or gray.

Printed fabric: A textile that features an image or motif created by the application of dye or pigment. Commercial techniques currently in use include roller printing, screen printing, and heat-transfer printing. Older methods include block printing and batiking.

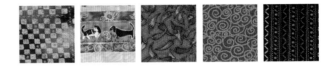

Fabrics in a variety of prints

Rhythm: A flow or sense of movement characterized by a basically regular repeat of elements or features, such as hue, value, intensity, or proportion. Rhythm is an important visual element when working with color and design.

Secondary colors: Colors created by mixing two primary colors: orange (red and yellow), green (yellow and blue), and violet (blue and red).

Shade: The resulting change in the intensity of a pure color created by the addition of black. Shades are darker in value than the pure color.

Spectral colors: Colors that appear when white light is diffracted through a prism. Violet, indigo, blue, green, yellow, orange, and red are the dominant spectral colors in the rainbow.

Split complementary: A three-color scheme created by combining a single color with the two colors adjacent to its complement, for example, yellow, red-violet, and blue-violet (the latter being the colors on either side of violet, yellow's complement).

Split complementary color scheme

Temperature: A "visual" characteristic of color. Some colors (suggesting water, sky, etc.) appear cool, whereas others (suggesting sun, fire, etc.) appear warm. The traditional color wheel is divided in half between the two, with the blues, greens, and violets composing the cool colors and the yellows, oranges, and reds composing the warm ones.

Tertiary colors: Colors created by mixing a primary and a secondary color, for example, yellow-orange (yellow and orange), blue-green (blue and green), and blue-violet (blue and violet). Also known as intermediary colors.

Tessellation: An arrangement or inlay of a single repeating shape—which can be as simple as a square—to create a mosaic pattern.

A tessellating pattern

Theme: The subject matter or starting point for a quilt. Quilt themes are often inspired by a particular piece (or collection) of fabric, also called a focus fabric. Patriotic, floral, pictorial, and juvenile are just a few possible themes.

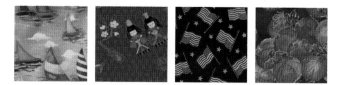

Theme or focus fabrics

Tint: The resulting change in the intensity of a pure color created by the addition of white. Tints are lighter in value than the pure color.

Tone: The resulting change in the intensity of a pure color made by adding gray. Tones are darker in value than the pure color.

Triadic: A color scheme based on three colors equidistant from each other on the color wheel, for example, yellow, blue, and red; orange, green, and violet.

Triadic color scheme

Value: The relative lightness or darkness of a color.

These fabrics reflect a wide range of value—light to dark—in a single color.

Warm colors: The yellow, orange, and red members of the color wheel. (Yellow is the strongest color on the color wheel and one of my favorites!) These colors are stimulating and powerful; they suggest sunlight, flames, and fall foliage. Warm colors typically advance into the foreground of a design.

Fabrics in warm colors

White: The lightest of the neutrals and the opposite of black. The color of radiated, transmitted, or reflected light containing all the visible rays of the spectrum. In our culture, white is associated with innocence, babies, and brides.

Woven design: A pattern produced in fabric by using a specific sequence of different-colored yarns in the warp and weft, for example, the traditional houndstooth pattern. Other woven designs identified by color include plaids, stripes, ikats, and dobby patterns.

COLOR RULES: *Learn them to break them!*

The Color Wheel

In 1666, a 23-year-old student named Isaac Newton found himself home from Cambridge, quarantined while the plague swept England. During this period, Newton discovered that by passing a light through a glass prism he could duplicate—in order—the colors of the rainbow: red, orange, yellow, green, blue, indigo, and violet. Although he discovered an infinite number of colors in the spectrum, he focused on these seven main (or spectral) colors. He compared his discovery to the seven musical notes in the diatonic scale and to the seven known planets. This became the basis for what we now know as the color wheel.

> ### SIR ISAAC NEWTON:
> *He's the father of the color wheel—
> and also my favorite famous guy.
> We share the same birthday!*

The color wheel most quilters are familiar with is a twelve-step color wheel that includes the three primary colors, the three secondary colors, and the six tertiary or intermediate colors. Yellow always appears at the top center position.

The color wheel is a useful tool that guides the way to a better understanding of color relationships by making them visual. The relationships—for example, across the color wheel (complementary), analogous (side by side on the color wheel), and triadic (three equally spaced colors on the color wheel)—are easy to identify. Through observation and practice, you will find the color wheel an infinite source of successful color schemes for your quilts.

GET CREATIVE!

Note: I've included a mix of exercises throughout the book to help you further explore the various lessons about color and design and to give you the opportunity to let your creativity soar. Here is the first. Have fun!

This exercise will help you become more familiar with the color wheel and the pure colors that "live" there. It will also help you become more acquainted with the fabrics in your stash and to identify quickly any particular color families you may be lacking.

Photocopy the color wheel outline on page 10 onto sturdy white paper. Make two copies. Trace one "wedge" onto template plastic, and use the template to cut out one example of each color named on the wheel from the fabrics in your stash. Use a glue stick to position the fabric wedge in its proper place. Refer to the color wheels below to be sure you are selecting a fabric that reflects the pure color or hue.

Make two color wheels: one entirely from solid (unprinted) fabrics and one entirely from prints.

Two color wheels made with fabric: one with solids and one with prints

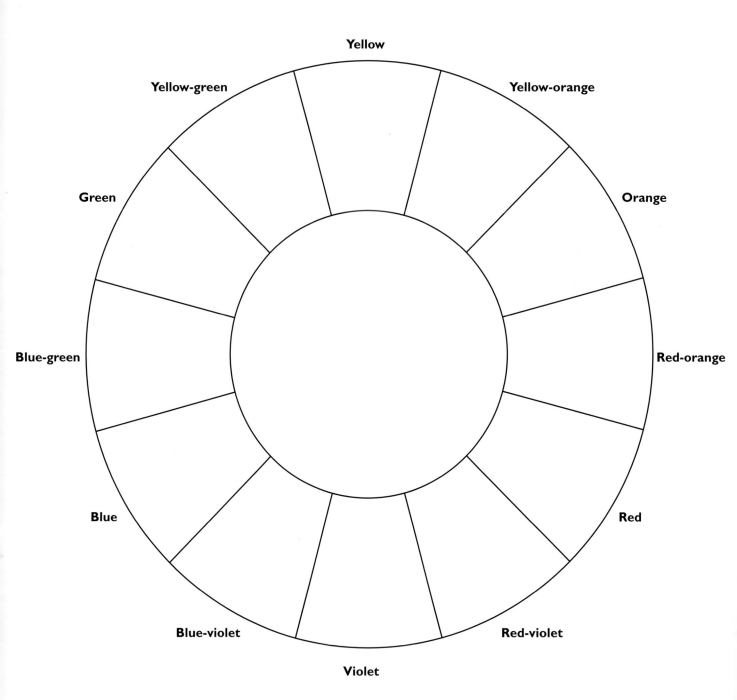

Color wheel outline—Make two copies.

In the beginning, there was color! Color attracts us, color communicates with us, and color is power! Here are some thoughts, attitudes, and superstitions associated with the primary and secondary colors.

Red

Red, a primary color, energizes, stimulates, and draws our attention. It is the color of fire, associated with warmth, with strength, and with fame. It appears in the flags of many nations.

Red is used extensively in advertising, especially—since it stimulates hunger—in advertisements concerning food and places to purchase and consume it.

In China, red is considered a particularly auspicious color and is traditionally worn by a bride on her wedding day.

Roses, tulips, strawberries, raspberries, and watermelons, claim the color red. Many sweethearts receive red roses, so red is often considered the color of love and passion.

Yellow

Primary yellow is the brightest and lightest color in the color world—and on the color wheel. It is a color of spring and summer, of daffodils, dandelions, sunflowers, and corn on the cob.

Yellow is warm, brilliant, and glowing—the color of the sun, the energy source for our planet.

For generations worn only by emperors, kings, or queens, yellow represents power, patience, and tolerance. Crests, religious symbols, dragons, and imperial emblems were embroidered onto royal clothing with threads of gold.

Blue

The third primary color—blue—is a most popular color. We live in blue houses, we drive blue cars, and we sing the blues!

The color of harmony and peace, blue is known to have a calming effect. A blue living room or bedroom beckons as a retreat, a place to relax. This serene color is used widely in hospitals and other similar institutions.

Aristocrats are known as "blue bloods," and many in the working class are known as "blue collar." Win first place in a competition and you receive a blue ribbon. Baby boys wear baby blue!

In the world of fashion, navy blue is sophisticated and slenderizing, and who among us has never worn a pair of blue jeans?

Purple

Envision the secondary color purple, a cool blend of red and blue. It is impulsive, passionate, and sensual—a medley of lavenders, lilacs, Italian plums, and French cabernet!

Purple or violet inspire respect, and once only the royal, the noble, or the religious were permitted to wear this imperial color. Priests wore rings set with amethyst (a purple semiprecious stone) to remind them not to overeat!

In some cultures, purple is also a color of mourning—or "half-mourning." After an appropriate period of time, widows of the nineteenth century traditionally moved from wearing black to wearing purple garments before returning to "normal" life.

Green

Green, a secondary color that combines blue and yellow, represents freshness, hope, birth, tranquility, and the joys of youth! It is a bright, powerful, and intelligent color—the color of spring.

On the other hand, you can be "green with envy" or have a "sickly green-colored" skin.

I like to think of green as the symbol of balance and of our environment, Mother Earth. It calls to mind deep rich forests, lush fields, St. Patrick's Day, and, of course, the "Emerald City" of the Northwest—Seattle!

Orange

Orange, a secondary color, is a strong, vital mix of red and yellow. A warm color, it is the color of transition and suggests the heat of a midsummer day, autumn foliage, brightly colored fish, and romantic, glowing embers. Envision lush tropical fruits—oranges, cantaloupes, and papayas—and rich winter vegetables—pumpkins, carrots, and squash—and don't forget Cheetos!

Other than a brief appearance in the 1960s (and worn only by Twiggy), orange has never been in contention for color of the year. Not many of us drive orange cars, live in orange houses, or wear clothes of this happy color. Nevertheless, I believe orange to be a positive, cheerfully extroverted, and contemporary color.

Fabrics and Supplies

FABRIC

Each chapter includes guidance in choosing the fabrics that will help you tell a particular color or design story. When it comes to fabric in general, however, I'm a purist. I prefer to use 100% cotton fabric in my quilts.

Because I don't want any surprises *after* my quilt is finished, I prewash all new fabric before it goes on the shelf. I wash fat quarters in the sink and ½ yard and larger pieces in the washing machine. My husband, Michael, does the ironing as soon as the fabric comes out of the dryer, and I square up the pieces (with the help of our daughter Adrienne when she is home from college) as described on page 71. Then I know my fabric is ready to go when I am!

> **SO REALLY...** *what's your favorite color? It's a great place to start as you build your fabric stash. This could be your "quilter's neutral!"*

SUPPLIES

You don't need a lot of fancy gadgets or special equipment to complete the color exercises or to make the wonderful quilts in this book. The basics, including typical rotary supplies, work perfectly. Here is a list of what you'll need, with thoughts about my personal favorite features:

Rotary cutter: Make sure it has an ergonomic-style grip and reliable safety catch.

Cutting mat: This is a green mat with a grid. Lines marking the 45° angle are helpful.

Acrylic rulers: I suggest both the 6" x 24" and 6" x 12" sizes, preferably with the 45° angle indicated.

Ruler grips: The clear type is best. These adhesive tabs stick to the bottom of your rulers to keep them from slipping as you cut.

Pins: Fine, glass-head silk pins don't leave unsightly holes in the fabric.

Scissors: Make sure you have both fabric scissors and small embroidery-type scissors for cutting thread.

Seam ripper: Use one with an ergonomic-style handle.

Thread: 100% cotton thread in a neutral color is best for piecing.

Glue stick: The water-soluble type comes in handy for securing embellishments before sewing. You'll also use it for various creativity exercises.

Sewing machine needles: Keep a good supply on hand to change after each project.

Sewing machine: Make sure your machine is in good working order, with a ¼-inch presser foot to help keep piecing accurate. If your machine does not come with this foot, I strongly recommend that you buy one!

Additional attachments: If you plan to machine quilt and apply binding by machine, a dual-feed or walking foot is a must for straight-line quilting. A darning foot or open-toe foot is useful for free-motion quilting; and for attaching trims, a cording or braiding foot makes the job go much more smoothly. For more information on these feet as they apply to machine quilting, see page 70.

From left to right: arrow braid/cord foot, braiding foot, open-toe (darning) foot, and dual-feed (walking) foot

YOUR CREATIVITY NOTEBOOK

As I mentioned on page 9, this book is sprinkled with exercises for developing your color and design awareness and for stretching your design sensibility. You'll also be encouraged to explore your responses to the various lessons. No doubt, you'll want one central place to keep all of this material, both as a chronicle of your personal journey and as a valuable reference for future quiltmaking projects.

As I began guiding my trusty group of quilters through the lessons that became the basis for this book, I had them begin a Creativity Notebook—and I strongly suggest that you start one as well. You can find everything you need at your local office supply store.

A simple 8½" x 11", three-ring binder is ideal, as it allows you to add or remove pages and gives you lots of flexibility in regard to content. You'll want a mix of lined and unlined, hole-punched 8½" x 11" paper: lined for making notes and journaling; unlined for sketches, collages, and other creative items. Add a couple of plastic page protectors and sleeve pockets for blocks, fabric swatches, and other miscellaneous odds and ends. Decorate the cover if you wish, insert the two color wheels you've already made (page 9), and you are on your way!

CREATIVITY

Creativity is the essence of life. Creating and re-creating keeps us vital—whether we are painting our home, planting a garden, or making a quilt.

Look at your quilt as your life's adventure. Imagine the entire process: selecting the fabric, constructing the top, making decisions about the quilting motifs. Stay alert, involved, and open as the quilt emerges. Opportunities will continue to present themselves at each step of the process.

Be an observer. Observation is an important element in creativity. Consider color and design in a new way; take a moment to think about your quilt. Opening yourself to creativity makes you even more creative. You are experiencing the process of invention with every quilt you make.

Each quilter brings his or her own life experience to a quilt. Each looks at fabric, color, and pattern in a different way. An artist sees things with a different perspective. With imagination and passion, your creativity will flourish.

The creative process leads to innovation and inspires us to be better quilters. Give yourself permission to be creative, to take a moment to wonder, to dream, to grow.

Consider a life—a quilt—based on creativity. Nothing ventured, nothing gained.

Pages from Creativity Notebooks kept by M'Liss's quilters

Making the
Century of Progress
Block

Are you ready to begin a wonderful journey? Each of the following chapters covers a different color or design scheme or "story" and includes a quilt—based on the Century of Progress block—that allows you to experiment with the lesson taught.

The makeup, the measurements, and the construction of each quilt are quite simple. The basic block finishes 8 inches. The basic quilt, is made up of six blocks—two blocks across by three blocks down. All of the other quilts are simply variations on this basic plan.

The Century of Progress block has nine pieces: rectangles, strips, and a square. The block is constructed the same way, and the nine elements remain in the same position even when the block is modified—for example, changed in proportion—for any particular quilt.

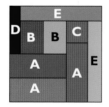

Century of Progress block

You will cut each piece from a different fabric; it's important to have a range of value, as well as variety, in the type and scale of the prints.

> **WARM UP!** *To get the hang of it, make one block before you cut out the entire quilt.*

MAKING A BLOCK

Cut all pieces across the fabric width (selvage to selvage).

To make one 8" Century of Progress block:

Cut 3 pieces 2½" x 5½" (A).

Cut 2 pieces 2½" x 3½" (B).

Cut 1 piece 2½" x 2½" (C).

Cut 1 piece 1½" x 4½" (D).

Cut 2 pieces 1½" x 7½" (E).

1. Stitch 2 A pieces together; press.

2. Stitch the B pieces together; press.

3. Stitch the remaining A piece to the C square; press.

4. Stitch 1 E strip to the unit from Step 3; press.

5. Stitch the D strip to the unit from Step 2, stopping 1" from the top of the unit; press.

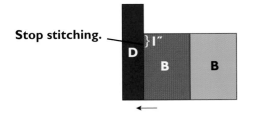

6. Stitch the unit from Step 5 to the top of the unit from Step 1; press.

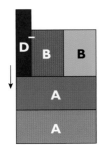

7. Stitch the unit from Step 6 to the left side of the unit from Step 4; press.

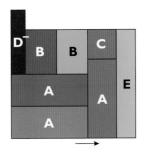

8. Stitch the remaining E strip to the top of the unit from Step 7, keeping the D strip free; press.

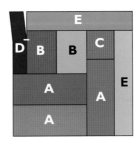

9. Finish stitching the partial seam between D and the unit from Step 8 to complete the block; press.

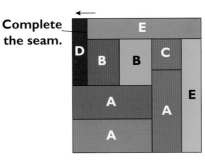

The Lessons

In the first lesson, you will explore a color story that focuses on the absence of color and work exclusively with white, gray, and black fabrics. You will continue with lessons that gradually introduce color and are designed to increase your knowledge of color theory and push you forward creatively. Bring along your sense of adventure—and lots of fabric. This is going to be fun!

The Achromatic Color Story

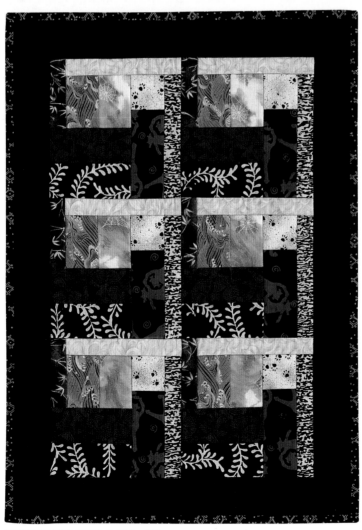

ACHROMATIC OPUS 1, 21" x 29",
pieced and machine quilted by M'Liss Rae Hawley, 2001.

As evening approaches and the sun sets, darkness eliminates color and all we see are shades and tones of black and gray...

Achromatic refers to the absence of color. When you work in an achromatic color scheme, you are working exclusively with the true neutrals of white, gray, and black.

Surprisingly, you may find the achromatic color story the most challenging one to master. As quilters, we are so connected to color that the mere thought of making a quilt without color can be very difficult—and threatening. But don't be afraid to give it a try; the experience is so valuable and so worthwhile! Working without color is a challenge that will push you to more creativity. To tell this color story, you must rely on visual texture, scale of pattern, and, most important, value.

These fabrics show the subtle addition of other dye colors. They are not true grays.

These fabrics introduce color in the printed motifs and therefore are not achromatic.

THE QUILT

Finished quilt size: 21½" x 29½"

Finished block size: 8"

Number of blocks: 6

You may choose to make six identical blocks, placing the same fabrics in the same position in each block as I have done in *Achromatic Opus 1* (page 16).

I made all blocks identical for Achromatic Opus 1.

For a greater challenge, make each block from a different group of fabrics. You won't need as much of any one fabric, but you'll need a greater number of fabrics to choose from. Just keep the placement of value basically the same in each one.

Photocopy the block diagram on page 18 to experiment with the placement of the light, medium, and dark fabrics before you cut the fabric pieces. Refer to Quiltmaking Basics (pages 67–73) as needed for guidance with general quiltmaking techniques.

MATERIALS

Yardages are based on fabric that measures 40" wide after laundering.

¼ yard (or fat quarter) of 9 different white, gray, and black fabrics for blocks

½ yard black subtle print for border

½ yard black-and-white print for binding

¾ yard for backing

29" x 37" piece of batting

CUTTING THE BORDERS AND BINDING

Cut all strips across the fabric width (selvage to selvage).

From border fabric
Cut 4 strips 3" x 40".

From binding fabric
Cut 3 strips 3" x 40".

ASSEMBLY

1. Refer to Making the Century of Progress Block (pages 14–15) to cut and construct six 8" Century of Progress blocks. Use the assorted white, black, and gray fabrics.

2. Arrange the blocks in 3 horizontal rows of 2 blocks each.

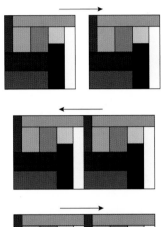

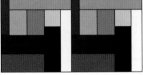

3. Sew the blocks together into rows. Press the seams in alternating directions from row to row.

4. Sew the rows together; press.

5. Refer to Adding Borders (pages 68-69). Measure, trim, and sew a 3"-wide border strip to the top, bottom, and sides of the quilt. Press the seams toward the border.

FINISHING

1. Refer to Preparing Your Quilt for Quilting (page 69). Layer the quilt top, batting, and backing; baste.

2. Hand or machine quilt as desired. Trim the batting and backing.

3. Use the 3"-wide black-and-white print strips to bind the quilt edges.

4. Add a hanging sleeve, and label if desired.

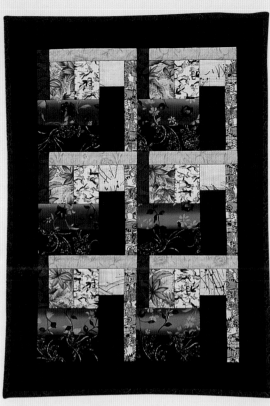

Silhouettes, *21" x 28"*,
pieced and machine quilted by Vicki DeGraaf, 2004.

Photocopy and use this block to experiment with the placement of light, medium, and dark values. Note: Block not full size.

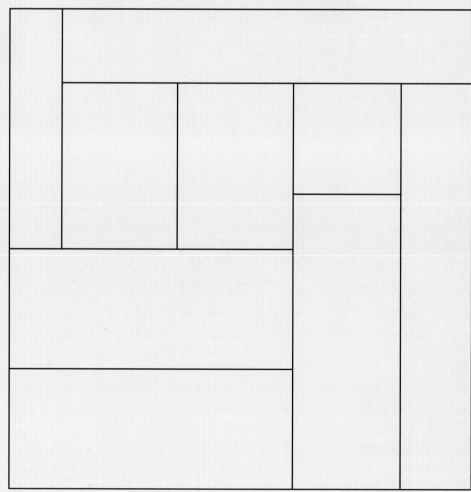

The
Monochromatic
Color Story

ROSÉ ON POINT, *32½" x 43½", pieced by M'Liss Rae Hawley.*
Machine quilted by Barbara Dau, 2004.

The word "monochromatic" comes from the Greek words *monos* ("single") and *chroma* ("color"). A quilt made entirely with fabrics of a single color—including all of its various tints, tones, and shades— is a monochromatic quilt. The range of value in a monochromatic quilt is the same as that of an achromatic quilt, but with all the tints, tones, and shades of a single color used in place of white, gray, and black.

Depending on the fabrics you choose, a monochromatic quilt can be traditional or "arty," sophisticated or playful—but always fun to make!

EYES OPEN! *Just as when you selected fabrics to tell your achromatic story, you'll need to be extremely watchful when choosing fabrics for your monochromatic quilt. A fabric can be considered truly monochromatic—and a suitable candidate for a monochromatic quilt—only when it is free from any other color. A green leaf on a red flower is not red—and the resulting fabric isn't either!*

The fabric on the left is not suitable for a monochromatic quilt. The one on the right is!

THE QUILT

Finished quilt size: 32 1/8" x 43 1/2"

Finished block size: 8"

Number of blocks: 6

Select one color you wish to work with. For my monochromatic quilt *Rosé on Point*, I chose red, beginning with its lightest value—pink. Pink is simply a tint of red, that is, red with white added to the pure hue. The more white you add, the lighter the pink. To achieve a full range of value, I made sure to move in the other direction as well, adding the darker values of red to my mix. The darkest shades of red are deep burgundy, or red with black added to the pure color.

I chose reds ranging in value from pink to burgundy for Rosé on Point.

Photocopy the block diagram on page 18 to experiment with the placement of the light, medium, and dark fabrics in the block before you cut the fabric pieces.

As with the quilt in the achromatic lesson, you may choose to make six identical blocks, placing the same fabrics in the same position, as I did in *Rosé on Point* (page 19) and in *Evening in Asia* (page 22). Or, to stretch yourself further, make each block from a different group of fabrics. You won't need as much of any one fabric, but you'll need a greater number of fabrics to choose from. Whichever color or approach you choose, bring along the lessons you've learned from the previous "story" about visual texture and scale of pattern as well as value.

Refer to Quiltmaking Basics (pages 67–73) as needed for guidance with general quiltmaking techniques.

GET CREATIVE!

When you select your color for this lesson—let's say purple—think about why you made that choice, and jot down your reasons in your Creativity Notebook. Something as simple as the fact that you already own a lot of purple fabric is a perfectly fine reason. Your thoughts might examine why you purchased all that purple fabric to begin with!

Next, make a small collage that features your chosen color. On an unlined piece of 8½" x 11" paper, arrange and glue photos, postcards, magazine clippings, advertisements, bits of colored paper, or ribbons—anything that suggests your chosen color to you. Stitch colored thread and trims directly onto the paper; stitch or glue on buttons and charms. In other words, let your imagination soar! Add your collage to your Creativity Notebook.

MATERIALS

Yardages are based on fabric that measures 40″ wide after laundering.

¼ yard (or fat quarter) of 9 different fabrics in a single color for blocks

⅔ yard light-medium print for corner and setting triangles and setting squares

⅞ yard dark subtle print for border

½ yard dark print for binding

1½ yards for backing

40″ x 51″ piece of batting

CUTTING THE CORNER AND SETTING TRIANGLES AND SETTING SQUARES, BORDERS, AND BINDING

Cut all strips across fabric width (selvage to selvage).

From triangle and setting square fabric

Cut 2 squares 12⅝″ x 12⅝″. Cut twice diagonally to make 4 quarter-square setting triangles (8 total). You will need 6 triangles and will have 2 triangles left over.

Cut 2 squares 6⅝″ x 6⅝″. Cut once diagonally to make 2 half-square corner triangles (4 total).

Cut 2 setting squares 8½″ x 8½″.

From border fabric
Cut 5 strips 5″ x 40″.

From binding fabric
Cut 3 strips 3″ x 40″.

ASSEMBLY

1. Refer to Making the Century of Progress Block (pages 14–15) to cut and construct six 8″ Century of Progress blocks. Use the assorted ¼-yard pieces of fabric in your chosen color.

2. Arrange the blocks, setting squares, and setting triangles in diagonal rows.

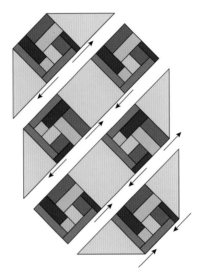

> ### TWIST AND TURN!
> *I gave the blocks in the middle row of both my monochromatic quilts a quarter turn for visual variety. Experiment with your blocks until you find an effect that pleases you.*

3. Sew the blocks, setting squares, and side setting triangles together into diagonal rows. Press the seams away from the pieced blocks.

4. Trim the "dog ears" at each corner. Sew the corner triangles to the quilt. Press the seams toward the triangles.

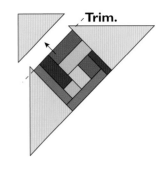

5. Square up the quilt top, making sure to leave a ¼″ seam allowance on all sides of the quilt.

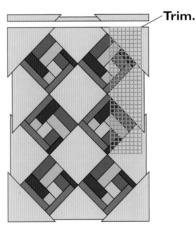

6. Refer to Adding Borders (pages 68-69). Measure, trim, and sew a 5″-wide border strip to the top and bottom of the quilt. Press the seams toward the border. Repeat to sew 5″-wide borders to the sides, piecing them as necessary; press.

> ### DO YOU HAVE A FAVORITE COLOR?
> *Expand your horizons! Collect more fabrics in your favorite, focusing on a range of values, textures, and scale of prints.*

FINISHING

1. Refer to Preparing Your Quilt for Quilting (page 69). Layer the quilt top, batting, and backing; baste.

2. Hand or machine quilt as desired. Trim the batting and backing.

3. Use the 3"-wide dark print strips to bind the quilt edges.

4. Add a hanging sleeve and label, if desired.

IT'S TRUE!

Yellow is the lightest and brightest color on the color wheel. You may have heard the common refrains: "Use yellow only in small quantities" or "Use yellow only as an accent color" —to which I say, NOT! Use yellow as the background color, as the key color of your theme fabric, or as the only color in a light, bright, and lovely monochromatic quilt.

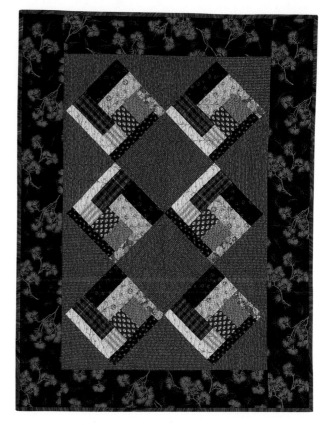

Evening in Asia, *32½" x 43½", pieced by M'Liss Rae Hawley. Machine quilted by Barbara Dau, 2001.*

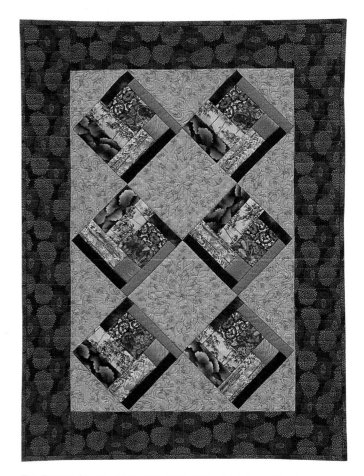

The Zen of Green, *32" x 42", pieced by Anastasia Riordan. Machine quilted by Barbara Dau, 2004.*

Banana Cream Pie, *32" x 44",*
pieced by Annette Barca.
Machine quilted by Barbara Dau, 2004.

Orange Slices and Licorice Drops,
29" x 40", pieced by Annette Barca.
Machine quilted by Barbara Dau, 2004.

The Complementary Color Story

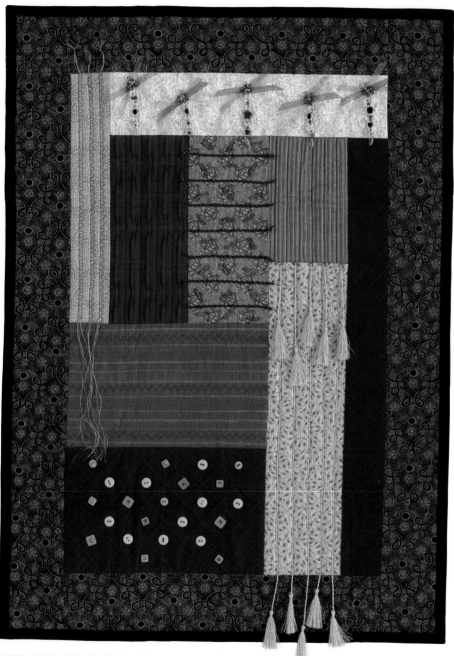

No doubt you've often heard the expression "opposites attract." That is certainly true when it comes to the colors on the color wheel. Color schemes based on colors directly opposite each other on the color wheel work because each color balances (or completes) the other. These two-color schemes are therefore called—surprise!—complementary.

If you look at the twelve-step color wheels you made (page 9), you will discover that the six complementary pairs include yellow and violet, yellow-green and red-violet, green and red, blue-green and red-orange, blue and orange, and blue-violet and yellow-orange.

INTERLUDE IN CHARTREUSE AND RED VIOLET, *22" x 30"*, *pieced, machine quilted, and embellished by M'Liss Rae Hawley, 2004.*

You do not need to restrict yourself to one-color fabrics when you work in a complementary color scheme. If you choose to work with the complementary pair of yellow and violet, some of your fabrics might be entirely yellow or violet, but others can be a mix of the two colors: perhaps a yellow star on a violet background.

These fabrics demonstrate the complementary color story of yellow and violet.

Because of your own color preferences (or prejudices), you may find that some complementary color pairs feel more comfortable to you than others, and you naturally gravitate toward these combinations when choosing the colors for your quilts. Why not take this opportunity to play with a complementary scheme that in the past might have seemed awkward to you or that you might have made a point to avoid? After all, isn't that what learning is all about? Remember, when complements are used in unequal proportions, a complementary scheme is always successful.

THE QUILT

Finished size: 22½" x 30½"

Finished block size: 16" x 24"

Number of blocks: 1

Select two colors directly across from each other on the color wheel—a complementary pair. As with the monochromatic story we explored in the previous chapter, you can expand your fabric options and add depth and drama to your quilt by using shades, tints, or tones of either or both colors.

I chose the pair of yellow-green and red-violet when I made *Interlude in Chartreuse and Red Violet* (page 24) to tell this color story. The block below, in which the two complements are red and green, demonstrates another example of a complementary scheme.

This 8" Century of Progress block features the complementary color scheme of red and green.

In addition to introducing a new color story, the quilt for this chapter teaches a lesson about proportion. The quilt is made from just one block, but here's the twist: you will change the proportion of the block so it is twice as wide and three times as long as the 8" version you've worked with so far. On the basis of the original 8" block, the ratio between the width of this block and its length is 2:3; the finished block measures 16" x 24". Wait until you see what a difference that makes, not just in the appearance of the block, but also in how the colors, values, and prints work. (For more on changing block proportions, see page 29.)

Photocopy the block diagram on page 28 to experiment with the placement of the colors and the light, medium, and dark values in the block before you cut the fabric pieces.

GET CREATIVE!

Consider adding texture and embellishment to the individual fabric pieces, either before or after you sew them together to construct the block. I enhanced *Interlude in Chartreuse* and *Red Violet* with decorative threads and stitches, pin tucks, couching, beads, and buttons. The results, I think, add a sophisticated touch to a simple design.

The possibilities for creativity are endless. Use threads and embellishments that blend with the fabrics for a tone-on-tone effect, or play up the complementary relationship by working with threads and embellishments in the opposite color. For some embellishing and fabric manipulation techniques—such as pin tucks (page 27)—you will want to cut the pieces larger than instructed and trim them to size after you have finished embellishing them. Use your Creativity Notebook to record any adjustments you make in cutting and piecing and any special needles, threads, and stitch settings you use. Use your notebook to keep any stitched or embellished samples.

For more on embellishment, see pages 74–76. In addition, you will find ideas and tips for adding texture to your quilts scattered throughout the book.

Refer to Quiltmaking Basics (pages 67–73) as needed for guidance with general quiltmaking techniques.

MATERIALS

Yardages are based on fabric that measures 40" wide after laundering.

¼ yard each of 9 different fabrics in 2 colors for blocks

½ yard for border

½ yard for binding

1 yard for backing

30½" x 38½" piece of batting

CUTTING

Cut all pieces and strips across the fabric width (selvage to selvage).

From the assorted fabrics in your chosen colors

Cut 1 piece 4½" x 15½" (A1).

Cut 2 pieces 6½" x 10½" (A2).

Cut 2 pieces 4½" x 9½" (B).

Cut 1 piece 4½" x 6½" (C).

Cut 1 piece 2½" x 12½" (D).

Cut 1 piece 3½" x 14½" (E1).

Cut 1 piece 2½" x 21½" (E2).

From border fabric

Cut 4 strips 3½" x 40".

From binding fabric

Cut 4 strips 3" x 40".

ASSEMBLY

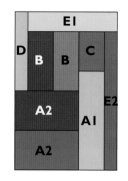

Block diagram

1. Refer to Making the Century of Progress Block (pages 14–15) and the block diagram above to construct one Century of Progress block. Use pieces A–E that you cut from your chosen colors. The unfinished block should measure 16½" x 24½".

2. Refer to Adding Borders (pages 68-69). Measure, trim, and sew a 3½"-wide border strip to the top, bottom, and sides of the quilt. Press the seams toward the border.

FINISHING

1. Refer to Preparing Your Quilt for Quilting (page 69). Layer the quilt top, batting, and backing; baste.

2. Hand or machine quilt as desired.

3. Use the 3"-wide strips to bind the quilt edges.

4. Add a hanging sleeve and label, if desired.

Making Pin Tucks

◆

Pin tucks are little channels created in the fabric when you stitch with twin needles and a special grooved foot. Pin tucks are a great way to enhance the surface of your quilt. They provide texture, added color, and a new twist on geometry and linear design. And here's good news: Pin tucks not only make your quilt more interesting, but they are also so easy to do!

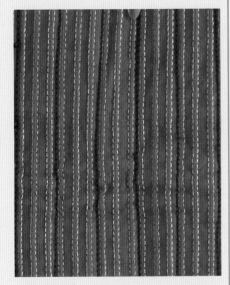

Pin tucks add dimension to this area of my quilt Interlude in Chartreuse and Red Violet. For a full view of this quilt, see page 24.

Because pin tucks gather the fabric slightly, you'll need to cut the piece you plan to embellish with pin tucks larger than the usual "finished measurement plus ¼" seam allowance." Plan on an extra ¼" of fabric for each ⅛" pin tuck. Experiment until you achieve just the look you want. Then include these "samples" in your Creativity Notebook!

In preparation for making pin tucks, you will need a five-groove, seven-groove, or nine-groove foot for your sewing machine.

Variety of grooved pin-tuck attachments

You will also need a twin or double needle with a distance between needles of 1.6mm to 2.0mm. Note that the wider the spacing between the needles, the larger the resulting tuck.

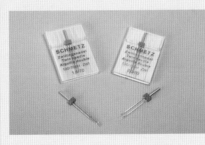

Twin needles suitable for making pin tucks

Place the pin-tuck foot on your sewing machine. Insert and thread the twin needle. The pin tucks are formed by the twin needles and thread as the fabric tunnels into the groove on the underside of the pin-tuck foot.

To make pin tucks—

1. Align the raw edge of the fabric piece with a throat plate marking to the right of the needle. This will help you keep the fabric (and first pin tuck) straight as you stitch.

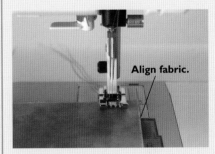

Machine and fabric ready for making pin tucks

2. Begin stitching. When you reach the end of the fabric, lift the needle, turn the fabric, and stitch in the opposite direction. Place the completed tuck in the outside groove of the foot to guide the next pin tuck. Continue until you've covered the desired area.

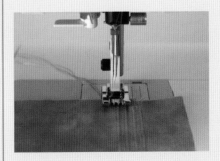

CREATIVE OPTIONS

◆ Use thread in contrasting colors or values in the twin needles.

◆ Embellish the pin-tucked area of your quilt with beading, trims, and decorative stitching.

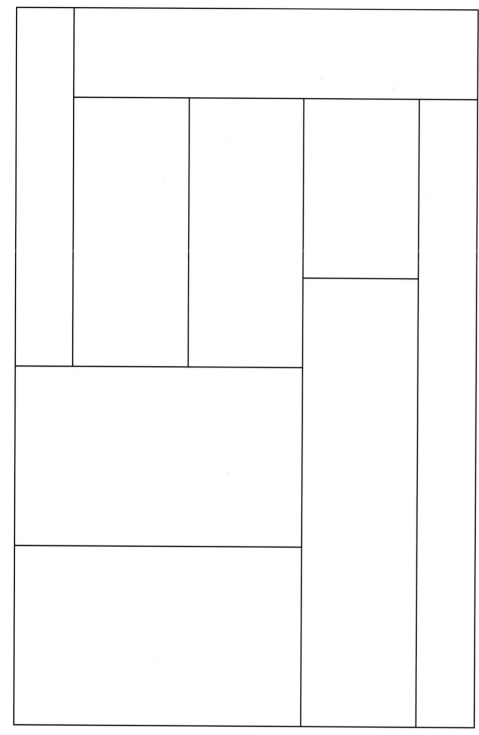

Photocopy and use this block to experiment with the placement of light, medium, and dark values. Note: Block not full size.

THE SPLIT COMPLEMENTARY STORY

A split complementary color scheme is a variation on the two-color complementary color scheme. This three-color scheme teams a single color with the colors on each side of its complement. (Your color wheel will be a huge help here!)

The split complementary combinations are yellow, blue-violet, and red-violet; yellow-green, violet, and red; green, red-violet, and red-orange; blue-green, red, and orange; blue, red-orange, and yellow-orange; blue-violet, orange, and yellow; violet, yellow-orange, and yellow-green; red-violet, yellow, and green; red, yellow-green, and blue-green; red-orange, green, and blue; orange, blue-green, and blue-violet; and yellow-orange, blue, and violet.

Many quilters do not care for these combinations at first sight, but I encourage you to give the split complementary color scheme a try, even if just in a single block. Once you have added the various tints, tones, and shades in a mix of pattern and scale, you will be surprised at how wonderful this color story can be. Don't forget the neutrals of white, gray, and black and the visual possibilities of embellishment: use them to help the colors blend.

This block demonstrates the split complementary scheme of yellow, blue-violet, and red-violet.

Changing the Block Proportions ◆

A ratio is the relationship in size, number, or degree between two or more similar things. Until this chapter, we have been working with a basic block that is traditionally square and that has a finished measurement of 8" x 8". The ratio between the sides is equal, or 1:1.

In this lesson, however, we changed the block proportions—and the resulting ratio (or relationship) between the block's width and length. Instead of 1:1, we used a block based on a ratio of 2:3. The first number refers to the finished width of the block and the second to its finished length. In this example, the block is twice the original 8" width and three times the original 8" length.

If you like the idea of changing the proportions of the block, here are some other ratios you might try. Measurements are based on an 8" x 8" block and reflect the finished block size. The diagrams illustrate the blocks and tell you how large to cut the pieces. Measurements for the individual pieces include ¼" seam allowances.

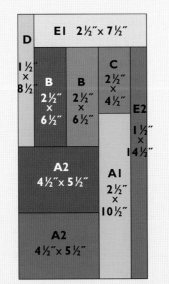

Ratio—1:2; Finished block—8" x 16"

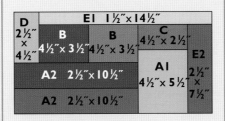

Ratio—2:1; Finished block—16" x 8"

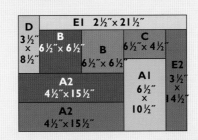

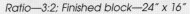

Ratio—3:2; Finished block—24" x 16"

RATIO	FINISHED BLOCK SIZE
1:2	8" x 16"
2:1	16" x 8"
3:2	24" x 16"
3:5	24" x 40"
4:2	32" x 16"
4:6	32" x 48"

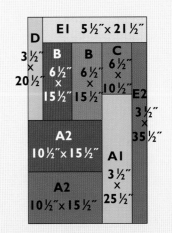

Ratio—3:5; Finished block—24" x 40"

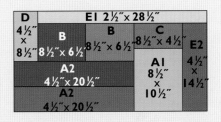

Ratio—4:2; Finished block—32" x 16"

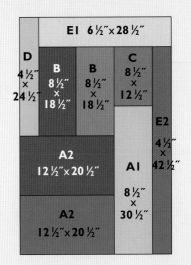

Ratio—4:6; Finished block—32" x 48"

A Little Bit of Sparkle, *22" x 30", pieced, embellished, and machine quilted by Susie Kincy, 2004.*

Machine Embellishment is Sew Much Fun!, *24" x 32", pieced, embellished, and machine quilted by Susie Kincy, 2004.*

I Think I Like It, 22" x 30",
pieced, embellished, and machine
quilted by Peggy Johnson, 2004.

Study in Purple and Yellow, 22½" x 30½",
pieced, machine quilted, and embellished
by Vicki DeGraaf, 2004.

The Triadic Color Story

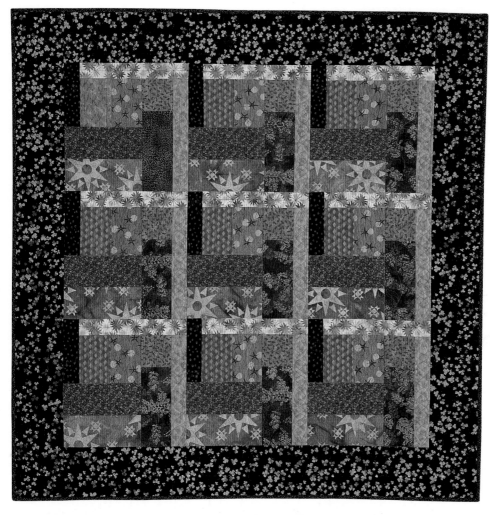

JESTER'S DANCE, *60" x 60", pieced by M'Liss Rae Hawley. Machine quilted by Barbara Dau, 2001.*

A triadic color scheme features three colors equally spaced from each other on the color wheel. Examples include the primary colors of yellow, red, and blue; the secondary colors of orange, violet, and green; and the tertiary combinations of yellow-orange, red-violet, and blue-green or red-orange, blue-violet, and yellow-green.

As with the complementary color scheme, you do not need to restrict yourself to one-color fabrics when you work in the triadic scheme. For example, if you choose to work with the orange-violet-green triad, some of your fabrics can be entirely green, orange, or violet—but others can mix any or all of the three colors. Just be careful not to let other colors slip into the mix!

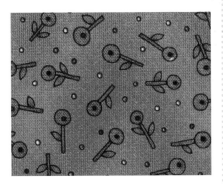

This fabric demonstrates the triadic color story of orange, violet, and green.

"I HATE THAT COLOR."

Have you ever said those words? Okay: You do not need to make a king-sized quilt all in orange fabric. Just give this happy color a try by introducing it in small proportions. You may be surprised!

THE QUILT

Finished quilt size: 60" x 60"

Finished block size: 16"

Number of blocks: 9

Choose three colors equally distant from each other on the color wheel—a triadic color scheme. For *Jester's Dance*, I chose the classic triad of orange, violet, and green. As you can see, I made sure to include a good mix of pattern and scale in the print fabrics for variety and visual excitement.

I chose a variety of prints with motifs in different sizes for the block in Jester's Dance.

For this quilt, you will double the size of the Century of Progress block, increasing it from an 8" to a 16" finished square. This larger size presents a wonderful challenge in working with color and scale. The overall block is not only twice the size, but each element (or shape) in the block is doubled as well. The enlarged proportions make everything more "obvious." You'll need to give extra thought to where you place the colors, values, and various prints.

You may choose to make nine identical blocks, placing the same fabrics in the same position, as I have done in *Jester's Dance* (page 32). For a bigger "stretch," make each block from a different group of fabrics. You won't need as much of any one fabric, but you'll need a greater number of fabrics to choose from. Whichever colors or approach you choose, bring along the lessons you've learned from the previous stories about visual texture and scale of pattern as well as value.

Photocopy the block diagram on page 18 to experiment with the placement of the light, medium, and dark fabrics in the block before you cut the fabric pieces.

Refer to Quiltmaking Basics (pages 67–73) as needed for guidance with general quiltmaking techniques.

GET CREATIVE!

Find swatches of any or all of the following: fabric, paper, wrapping paper, lengths of ribbon, photos, postcards, or magazine advertisements that demonstrate a triadic color story. Select just one of the triadic combinations (perhaps one you have not used for your quilt) or try to find examples for each of the four triadic combinations. Mount your examples in your Creativity Notebook.

While you're working in your notebook, jot down your thoughts on why you selected the triadic combination you chose for your quilt and what your expectations and feelings are for working with this color story.

MATERIALS

Yardages are based on fabric that measures 40" wide after laundering.

1/3 yard each of 12 different fabrics in 3 colors for blocks

1 1/2 yards for border

2/3 yard for binding

3 7/8 yards for backing

68" x 68" piece of batting

CUTTING

Cut all pieces and strips across the fabric width (selvage to selvage). You will use 3 A, 2 B, 1 C, 1 D, and 2 E in each block.

From the assorted fabrics in your chosen colors

Cut 27 pieces 4 1/2" x 10 1/2" (A).

Cut 18 pieces 4 1/2" x 6 1/2" (B).

Cut 9 pieces 4 1/2" x 4 1/2" (C).

Cut 9 pieces 2 1/2" x 8 1/2" (D).

Cut 18 pieces 2 1/2" x 14 1/2" (E).

From border fabric

Cut 7 strips 6 1/2" x 40".

From binding fabric

Cut 7 strips 3" x 40".

GET CREATIVE!

Make an 8" block duplicating the 16" block you're making for your triadic quilt. This will allow you to see how differently color, value, and scale of print "behave" when you change the size of the block and the elements in it. I'll bet you find the difference between blocks to be quite dramatic! Place the 8" block in your Creativity Notebook for future reference, along with your other notes and exercises on the triadic color scheme.

ASSEMBLY

1. Refer to Making the Century of Progress Block (pages 14–15) to construct nine 16" Century of Progress blocks. Use pieces A–E that you cut from your chosen colors.

2. Arrange the blocks in 3 horizontal rows of 3 blocks each.

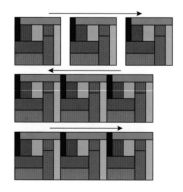

3. Sew the blocks together into rows. Press the seams in alternating directions from row to row.

4. Sew the rows together. Press.

5. Refer to Adding Borders (pages 68-69). Measure, trim, and sew a 6 1/2"-wide border strip to the top, bottom, and sides of the quilt, piecing them as necessary. Press the seams toward the border.

FINISHING

1. Refer to Preparing Your Quilt for Quilting (page 69). Layer the quilt top, batting, and backing; baste.

2. Hand or machine quilt as desired. Trim the batting and backing.

3. Use the 3"-wide strips to bind the quilt edges.

4. Add a hanging sleeve and label, if desired.

ALTERNATIVE QUILT SIZE

As you will see in the photographs on pages 35–36, some of the quilters in my group chose to make this quilt in slightly different sizes. One variation measures 44 1/2" x 60 1/2" and features 6 blocks in 3 horizontal rows of 2 blocks each. To try that option, adjust the cutting as follows:

Cut 18 A, 12 B, 6 C, 6 D, and 12 E. Cut 6 strips 6 1/2" x 40" for the border and 6 strips 3" x 40" for the binding. You will need a 52 1/2" x 68 1/2" piece of batting and 3 yards of fabric for backing.

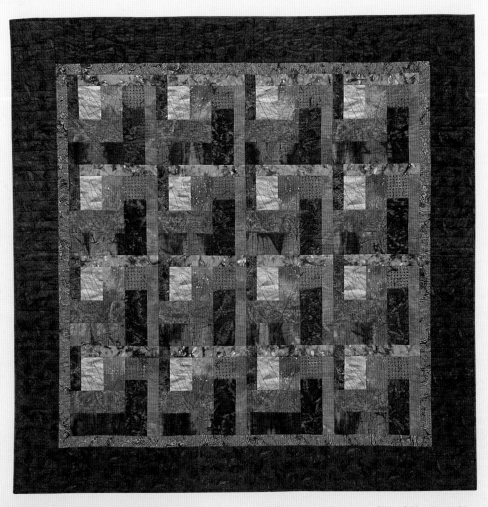

Secondary and Beyond, *84" x 84", pieced by Anastasia Riordan. Machine quilted by Barbara Dau, 2004.*

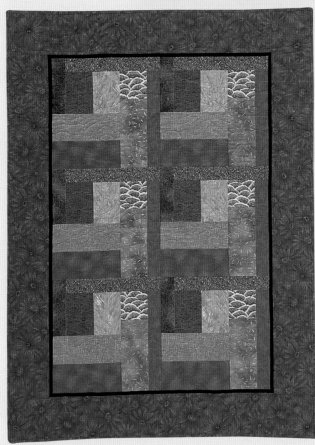

Harmony of Three, *44½" x 60", pieced and machine quilted by Stacie Johnson, 2004.*

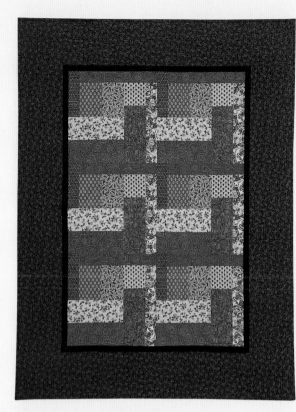

A Trip to Provence, *48½" x 64½",*
pieced by Susie Kincy. Machine quilted
by Barbara Dau, 2004.

Primary Colors—Mostly Yellow, *48" x 62", pieced by*
Vicki DeGraaf. Machine quilted by Susan Free, 2004.

Happy Times, *46½" x 62",*
pieced by Susie Kincy. Machine
quilted by Barbara Dau, 2004.

The Analogous Color Story

FOLLOW THE PATH—THE JOURNEY CONTINUES *(triptych)*,
*32" x 32", pieced, embellished, and machine quilted by
M'Liss Rae Hawley, 2004.*

Analogous colors are neighbors, appearing side by side on the color wheel. Examples of analogous color schemes include red, red-orange, and orange; orange, yellow-orange, and yellow; yellow, yellow-green and green; green, blue-green, and blue; blue, blue-violet, and violet; and violet, red-violet, and red. As you can see, there is a close relationship among the colors in an analogous scheme; the colors blend seamlessly from one to the next. It is hard to miss with a quilt based on this color story!

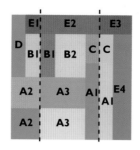

A single large Century of Progress block is the basis for this triptych.

THE QUILT

Finished overall size: 32" x 32"
(approximate)

Finished size of side panels:
8" x 32"

Finished size of center panel:
16" x 32"

Select three side-by-side colors on the color wheel to tell your analogous color story. Be sure to include tints, tones, and shades of the various colors, as well as a mix of pattern and scale in the fabrics you choose. As with the previous two lessons, remember also that some of the fabrics may include two or more of your chosen colors.

These fabrics demonstrate the analogous color scheme of blue, blue-violet, and violet.

The quilt you will use to tell this color story is unique. Rather than piecing a single large block or group of blocks, you will piece the quilt as three individual panels. This three-panel treatment is called a triptych. If you look closely, you will discover that a 32" x 32" version of the familiar Century of Progress block is the basis for this quilt.

I chose the analogous color scheme of yellow, yellow-green, and green for my triptych *Follow the Path—The Journey Continues* (page 37). I used threads in the same analogous colors to add machine embroidery and a tangle of tulle, ribbons, and other decorative fibers to "tie" the three pieces together. For more about the embellishment on this quilt—how and why I chose it and how I accomplished it—see pages 75–76.

Some of the quilters in my group used the triptych format to get creative with embellishment as well. Take particular note of Anastasia Riordan's *Expression in Mulberry* (page 41) and *My Aquarium* by Vicki DeGraaf (page 41).

My guess is that you too will find this a wonderful quilt to enhance with decorative stitching or other embellishment, either on the individual pieces before you sew them together or on the finished panels. You will find guidance and tips for successful machine embroidery on page 40. In addition, you will find ideas and tips for adding texture to your quilts scattered throughout the book. Use your Creativity Notebook to record any special threads, stabi-lizers, stitch settings, or other key information that you find helpful as you play.

Photocopy the diagram on page 42 to experiment with the placement of the colors and the light, medium, and dark values in the panels before you cut the fabric pieces.

Refer to Quiltmaking Basics (pages 67–73) as needed for guidance with general quiltmaking techniques.

GET CREATIVE!

Devote a page in your Creativity Notebook to your analogous color story. Your entry may address the source of inspiration for your analogous scheme, for the fabrics you have chosen to interpret it, or for the overall theme or design of your triptych. You can do this in any medium or combination of media, for example, with sketches, photography, collage, or stitchery. If you like, you can add text in the form of an original poem, short story, or journal entry.

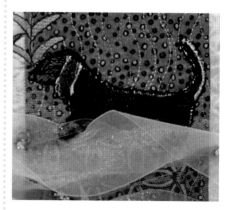

Detail of dachshund embroidery on Follow the Path—The Journey Continues.

MATERIALS

Yardages are based on fabric that measures 40" wide after laundering.

⅜ yard each of 16 different fabrics in 3 colors

¾ yard for binding

1¾ yards for backing

2 pieces of batting 16" x 40"

1 piece of batting 24" x 40"

CUTTING

Cut all pieces and strips across the fabric width (selvage to selvage).

From the assorted fabrics in your chosen colors*

Cut 2 pieces 4½" x 20½" (A1).

Cut 2 pieces 8½" x 8½" (A2).

Cut 2 pieces 8½" x 12½" (A3).

Cut 2 pieces 4½" x 12½" (B1).

Cut 1 piece 8½" x 12 ½" (B2).

Cut 2 pieces 4½" x 8½" (C).

Cut 1 piece 4½" x 16½" (D).

Cut 1 piece 4½" x 4½" (E1).

Cut 1 piece 4½" x 16½" (E2).

Cut 1 piece 4½" x 8½" (E3).

Cut 1 piece 4½" x 28½" (E4).

From binding fabric

Cut 8 strips 3" x 40".

From backing fabric

Cut 2 pieces 16½" x 40" across the fabric width.

Cut 1 piece 24½" x 40" across the fabric width.

*Cut each piece from a different fabric.

ASSEMBLY

Refer to the diagrams below to construct one of each side panel and one center panel. Use pieces A–E that you cut from your chosen colors.

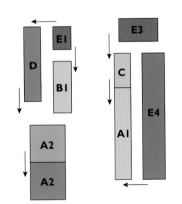

Side-panel diagrams

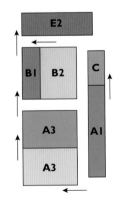

Center-panel diagram

FINISHING

1. Refer to Preparing Your Quilt for Quilting (page 69). Layer the panel tops, batting, and backing; baste.

2. Hand or machine quilt as desired. Trim the batting and backing.

3. Use the 3"-wide strips to bind the edges of each panel.

4. Add hanging sleeves and label, if desired.

THE TRIPTYCH: AN ALTERNATIVE APPROACH

If you prefer, you can make a single 32" x 32" Century of Progress block (page 55) and cut it into three sections (after piecing and quilting, but before binding) to create a triptych. Because you are piecing a single block, you will need only nine fabrics. Keep in mind that the panels will be a bit smaller; you lose seam allowances by dividing a single block.

You will need a single 40" x 40" piece of batting and 1⅛ yards of fabric for backing.

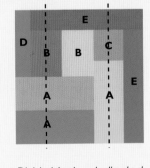

Divide block as indicated by dashed lines.

Machine Embroidery Tips

Machine embroidery offers an amazing opportunity to add beautiful layers of color and texture to your quilts. Here are some tips to help you get started:

◆ Prewash the fabric you plan to use as background for the embroidery designs. Washing will also preshrink the fabric—a necessary step!

◆ Begin with a fresh, new needle, and change it during the process if the point becomes dull. Skipped stitches are one indication of a dull needle. Some embroidery designs have an excess of 10,000 stitches. A dull needle can distort the design.

◆ Outfit your machine with an embroidery-foot attachment.

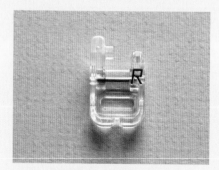

Embroidery foot

◆ Prewind several bobbins with polyester or cotton bobbin fill thread, such as Robison-Anton polyfilament bobbin thread. As an alternative, you can purchase prewound bobbins, such as those manufactured by Robison-Anton. Choose white or black, using the background fabric as your guide. You may want to change the bobbin thread as the color of the top thread changes.

◆ Select a fabric stabilizer to use under the fabric. There are many different types of stabilizers available; whichever you choose, read the manufacturer's instructions carefully. Some stabilizers are heat- or water-sensitive. I prefer a tear-away stabilizer, such as Inspira, Tear-Away Stabilizer, or Sulky of America's Tear Easy (medium weight), when I machine embroider on 100% cotton fabric. Sometimes a liquid stabilizer works well with a lightweight or light-colored fabric. If the fabric is prone to puckering, try a water- or heat-soluble stabilizer.

Examples of stabilizers

◆ A hoop is key; it keeps the fabric from shifting as you embroider the designs. If possible, place the fabric in the hoop so it is on the straight grain. Avoid puckers and pleats.

The fabric should be taut, but not pulled too tightly.

A hoop keeps fabric from shifting.

◆ The piece of the block or the section of the quilt you are working on may require extra width or length to fit in the hoop. Try stitching a piece of waste fabric to the edges. You can remove it when you have completed the embroidery.

◆ Stitch a test of the desired embroidery design, using the fabric, threads, and stabilizer you plan to use for the project. You will be able to tell whether the thread tension is correct, whether the thread coverage is sufficient, and how the embroidered design will look on the background fabric you've chosen, so you can make any necessary adjustments. If you wish, you can incorporate your test design into your label or quilt backing.

Expression in Mulberry, *32" x 32",
pieced, embellished, and machine
quilted by Anastasia Riordan, 2004.*

My Aquarium, *32" x 32", pieced,
embellished, and machine quilted by
Vicki DeGraaf, 2004.*

Photocopy and use this block to experiment with the placement of colors and light, medium, and dark values. Note: Block is not full size.

Sunset at Deception Pass, *32" x 32"*, *pieced by Annette Barca. Machine quilted by Barbara Dau, 2004.*

Telling Your Story Through Piecing: Following a Formula

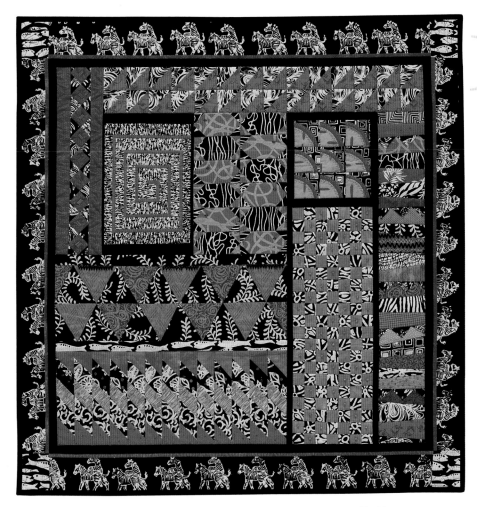

IN TRANSITION, 40½" x 40½", pieced, embellished, and machine quilted by M'Liss Rae Hawley, 2003.

Now that you've explored the key color stories, it's time to start looking at new, even more creative ways to tell them. You opened the door to "personal expression" when you made the triptych in the previous lesson. By exploring additional ideas for design, you are bound to discover countless other innovative ways to tell your story through your quiltmaking.

For this lesson—and in the two lessons that follow—you'll choose your own color story. Your color story may be inspired by a theme, such as a holiday; a special piece or collection of fabric (ethnic fabric, perhaps); something you see in nature; or a life event, celebration, or milestone. Check your Creativity Notebook; you may already have some inspiration there!

Once you've selected your color story, you'll use a variety of piecing techniques to express it.

THE QUILT

Finished quilt size: 40½" x 40½"

Finished block size: 32"

Number of blocks: 1

Select your color story based on your own personal inspiration. As always, include fabrics with variety in value and printed motif.

The quilt for this lesson is made from a single 32" (finished) Century of Progress block. By increasing the block to this larger size, you also substantially increase the size of each individual piece. These large individual pieces—or sections—are ideally sized for introducing a variety of piecing techniques to tell your personal story. That's what this lesson is all about.

My personal expression piece *In Transition* (page 43) was inspired by a series of changes in my life. I reduced my variables to include just one color—orange, the color of transition—that I teamed with the neutrals of black and white. The fabrics are a combination of batiks, hand dyes, and commercial print fabrics.

These are the fabrics I used for my quilt In Transition.

I pieced each section of the large block using a different technique. The instructions that follow describe making the quilt as I made it.

Refer to Quiltmaking Basics (pages 67–73) as needed for guidance with general quiltmaking techniques.

MATERIALS

Yardages are based on fabric that measures 40" wide after laundering.

⅓ yard each of 12–15 different fabrics in your colors and/or theme for the block sections*

¼ yard for corner squares

¼ yard for inner border

¼ yard for inset strip

⅝ yard for outer border

½ yard for binding

2¾ yards for backing

48" x 48" piece of batting

*These fabrics are described as orange, black, and white in the quilt instructions to match my quilt on page 43. Substitute fabrics in your chosen colors when constructing the various sections.

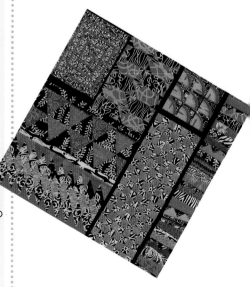

Cutting the Corner Squares, Borders, and Binding

Cut all pieces and strips across the fabric width (selvage to selvage).

From corner square fabric
Cut 4 squares 3¾" x 3¾".

From inner border fabric
Cut 4 strips 1¼" x 40".

From inset strip fabric
Cut 4 strips 1" x 40".

From outer border fabric
Cut 4 strips 3¾" x 40".

From binding fabric
Cut 5 strips 3" x 40".

	E1				
	Half-Square Triangles				
D	**B1**	**B2**	**C**		
Sem-	**Greek**	**Honey-**	**Quarter**		
inole	**Key**	**comb**	**Circles**		
Band		**Blocks**		**E2**	
	A2			**Stitch-**	
	Equilateral Triangles		**A1**	**ing**	
	A3		**Checker-**	**on**	
	Seminole Bias Strips		**board**	**Paper**	

Block diagram

Section A1: Checkerboard

Finished size: 8" x 20"

Cutting

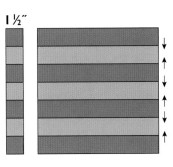

From orange fabric
Cut 7 strips
1½" x 20".

From black-and-white fabric
Cut 7 strips
1½" x 20".

From black fabric
Cut 2 strips
1" x 20½".

Assembly

1. Sew four 1½" x 20" black-and-white strips and three 1½" x 20" orange strips together, alternating them to make a strip set. Press.

Crosscut into 10 segments, each 1½" wide, squaring up the cut edge as needed.

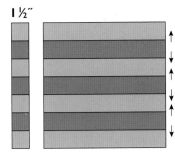

1½"

Cut 10.

2. Repeat Step 1 using 4 orange strips and 3 black-and-white strips. Crosscut into 10 segments, each 1½" wide, squaring up the cut edge as needed.

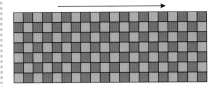

1½"

Cut 10.

3. Alternating the segments from Steps 1 and 2, sew them together to create a checkerboard. Press.

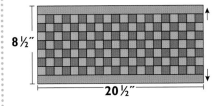

4. Sew the unit from Step 3 between two 1" x 20½" black strips. Press.

8½"

20½"

SECTION A2: EQUILATERAL TRIANGLES

Finished size: 8" x 20"

Cutting

From black fabric 1
Cut 2 strips 4" x 40".
Cut 1 strip 1½" x 22".

From orange fabric 1
Cut 1 strip 4" x 40".

From orange fabric 2
Cut 1 strip 4" x 40".

From black fabric 2
Cut 1 strip 1½" x 22".

Assembly

1. Carefully layer the 4" x 40" black fabric 1, orange fabric 1, and orange fabric 2 strips on your cutting mat. Position your ruler so that the 60° mark is aligned with the bottom edge of the strips. Cut along the edge of the ruler to remove the corner.

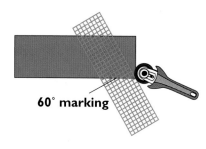

60° marking

2. Turn the strips so the cut edge is on the left. Place the ruler's 4" mark on the angled edge, and align the 60° mark along the bottom edges of the strips. Cut along the edge of the ruler. Cut 3 segments, each 4".

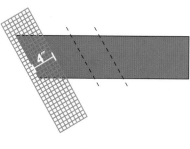

4"

Cut 3.

3. Cut the segments from Step 2 from corner to corner. (You can leave the segments stacked if you like.) You will have 12 black triangles and 6 each of the orange triangles. Stack the triangles by color, with the straight grain along the bottom edge.

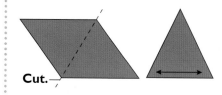

Cut.

4. Sew 12 triangles together to make a row, alternating black triangles with orange fabric 1 and orange fabric 2 triangles. Press. Make 1 of each row.

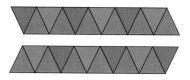

Make 1 of each.

5. Sew the rows together. Press. Sew the 1½" x 22" black fabric 1 strip to the top of the unit and the 1½" x 22" black fabric 2 strip to the bottom. Press. Trim the section to 8½" x 20½".

8½"

20½"

SECTION A3: SEMINOLE BIAS STRIPS

Finished size: 8" x 20"

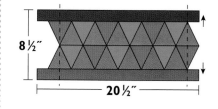

Cutting

From orange fabric 1
Cut 1 strip 1½" x 40".

From black fabric
Cut 2 strips 1¾" x 40".

From orange fabric 2
Cut 2 strips 2¼" x 40".

From muslin or other foundation fabric
Cut 1 rectangle 8" x 22".

Assembly

1. Sew the 40"-long strips together in the following order to make a strip set: orange fabric 2, black fabric, orange fabric 1, black fabric, and orange fabric 2. Press.

2. Position your ruler so that the 45° mark is aligned with the bottom edge of the strip set. Cut along the edge of the ruler to remove the corner. (Save this triangular piece; you may want to use it later.)

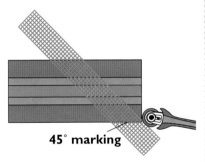

45° marking

3. Turn the strip set so the cut edge is on the left. Place the ruler's 2" mark on the angled edge, and align the 45° mark along the bottom edge of the strip set. Cut along the edge of the ruler. Cut 13 segments, each 2" wide, squaring up the cut edge as needed.

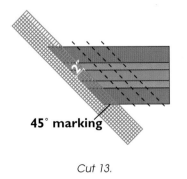

45° marking

Cut 13.

4. Place a segment from Step 3 right side up on the left edge of the 8" x 22" foundation piece. The top and bottom edges of the strip will overlap the foundation slightly. Stitch down the left edge of the strip with a 1/8"–3/16" seam allowance.

(The foundation fabric keeps the bias-cut strips from stretching out of shape.)

foundation fabric

5. Place a second strip over the first strip, with right sides together and the long raw edges even. (The seam allowances do not need to match.) Pin and sew using a scant 1/4" seam allowance. Open the second strip, and press.

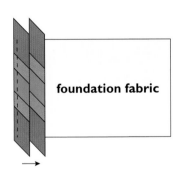

foundation fabric

6. Add the remaining strips as described in Step 5, checking occasionally to make sure the strips are straight. Take a deeper seam, if necessary, to maintain the integrity of the seam. Trim the section to 8½" x 20½".

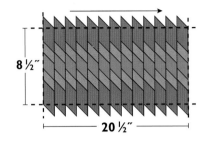

8 ½"

20 ½"

Section B1: Greek Key

Finished size: 8" x 12"

Cutting and Assembly

1. **From black fabric 1**
Cut piece 1, 1¼" x 1¾".

Cut piece 3, 1¼" x 2".

From orange fabric
Cut piece 2, ¾" x 1¼".

Cut piece 4, ¾" x 2".

2. Stitch pieces 1 and 2 together. Press. Add pieces 3 and 4 to create Unit A. Press.

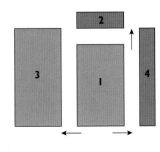

Unit A

3. **From orange fabric**

Cut piece 5, ¾" x 2¼".

Cut piece 7, ¾" x 3¼".

From black fabric 1

Cut piece 6, 1½" x 2¼".

Cut piece 8, 1¼" x 3¼".

4. Stitch pieces 5 and 6 to Unit A. Press. Add pieces 7 and 8 to create Unit B. Press.

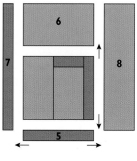

Unit B

5. **From black fabric 1**

Cut piece 9, 1½" x 3¼".

Cut piece 11, 1¼" x 4½".

From orange fabric

Cut piece 10, ¾" x 3¼".

Cut piece 12, ¾" x 4½".

6. Stitch pieces 9 and 10 to Unit B. Press. Add pieces 11 and 12 to create Unit C. Press.

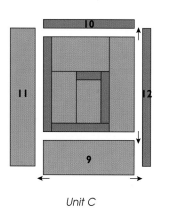

Unit C

7. **From orange fabric**

Cut piece 13, ¾" x 4 ¼".

Cut piece 15, ¾" x 5¾".

From black fabric 1

Cut piece 14, 1½" x 4¼".

Cut piece 16, 1¼" x 5¾".

8. Stitch pieces 13 and 14 to Unit C. Press. Add pieces 15 and 16 to create Unit D. Press.

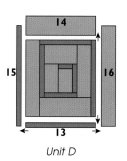

Unit D

9. **From black fabric 1**

Cut piece 17, 1½" x 5¼".

Cut piece 19, 1¼" x 7".

From orange fabric

Cut piece 18, ¾" x 5¼".

Cut piece 20, ¾" x 7".

10. Stitch pieces 17 and 18 to Unit D. Press. Add pieces 19 and 20 to create Unit E. Press.

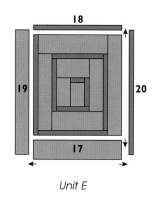

Unit E

11. **From orange fabric**

Cut piece 21, ¾" x 6¼".

Cut piece 23, ¾" x 8¼".

From black fabric 1

Cut piece 22, 1½" x 6¼".

Cut piece 24, 1¼" x 8¼".

12. Stitch pieces 21 and 22 to Unit E. Press. Add pieces 23 and 24 to create Unit F. Press.

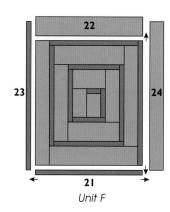

Unit F

13. **From black fabric 1**

Cut piece 25, 1½" x 7¼".

Cut piece 27, 1¼" x 9".

From orange fabric

Cut piece 26, ¾" x 7¼".

14. Stitch pieces 25 and 26 to Unit F. Press. Add piece 27 to create Unit G. Press.

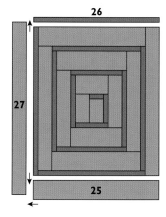

Unit G

15. **From black fabric 1**
Cut piece 28, 1½" x 8".

16. Stitch piece 28 to Unit G to create Unit H. Press.

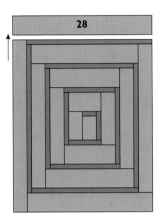

Unit H

17. **From black fabric 2**
Cut pieces 29 and 30, 1½" x 8" each.

Cut pieces 31 and 32, ¾" x 12½" each.

18. Stitch pieces 29 and 30 to Unit H. Press. Add pieces 31 and 32. Press.

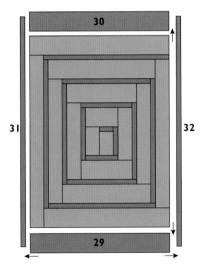

Completed Greek Key

SECTION B2: HONEYCOMB BLOCKS

Finished size: 8" x 12"

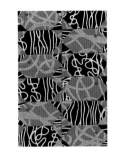

Cutting

From black fabric
Cut 6 rectangles 2½" x 4½".

Cut 24 squares 1½" x 1½".

From orange fabric
Cut 6 rectangles 2½" x 4½".

Cut 24 squares 1½" x 1½".

Assembly

1. Draw a diagonal line from corner to corner on the wrong side of each 1½" square. With right sides together, place a marked square on opposite corners of a 2½" x 4½" rectangle of the contrasting color. Stitch on the drawn lines. Cut away the excess fabric, leaving a ¼" seam allowance. Press. Repeat to sew 1½" squares to the remaining corners of each contrasting unit. Make 6 of each combination.

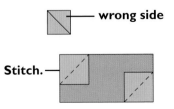

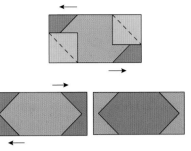

Make 6 of each.

2. Arrange segments from Step 1 in 2 columns of 6 units each. Sew the units together into columns. Press. Sew the columns together. Press.

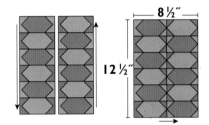

SECTION C: QUARTER CIRCLES

Finished size: 8" x 8"

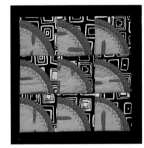

Cutting

From black fabric 1
Cut 3 squares 5½" x 5½".

From black fabric 2
Cut 2 strips 1¼" x 7¼".
Cut 2 strips 1¼" x 8¾".

Assembly

1. Make templates for the large and small circles using the patterns on page 52. Trace 3 large circles on orange fabric 1 and 3 small circles on orange fabric 2. Cut out on the drawn lines.

2. Center a large circle on a 5½" black fabric 1 square, and secure with fabric adhesive. Center a smaller circle on the larger circle, and secure.

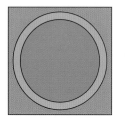

3. Finish the edges of the circles with a decorative machine stitch and a coordinating thread and tear-away stabilizer. (Using a walking foot helps keep the pieces flat.) Make sure the thread overlaps the edge of the fabric. Press from the wrong side. Make 3.

4. Cut each square from Step 3 into quarters. (Each quarter should measure 2¾" x 2¾".)

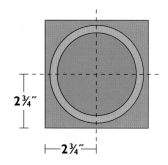

5. Arrange the units from Step 4 in 3 rows of 3 units each in a pleasing order. Sew the units into rows. Press. Sew the rows together. Press.

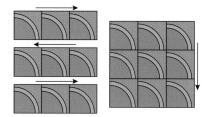

6. Sew a 1¼" x 7¼" black fabric 2 strip to each side of the unit from Step 5. Press. Sew a 1¼" x 8¾" black fabric 2 strip to the top and bottom. Press. Trim the section to 8½" x 8½".

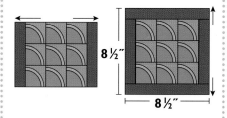

SECTION D: SEMINOLE BAND

Finished size: 4" x 16"

Cutting

From orange fabric
Cut 1 strip 1¾" x 40".
Cut 2 strips 1¾" x 18".

From black fabric
Cut 2 strips 2" x 40".

Assembly

1. Sew the 1¾" x 40" orange strip between the 2" x 40" black strips to make a strip set. Press. Crosscut into 16 segments, each 1¾". Square up the edges as needed.

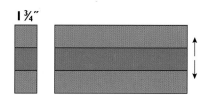

Cut 16.

2. Sew the segments together, staggering them and matching seam allowances. Press.

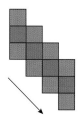

3. Trim the zigzag edges of the band, making sure to preserve a ¼" seam allowance. Press the band carefully using spray starch. Save the trimmed edges; you may want to use them later.

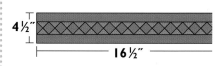

4. Sew a 1¾" x 18" orange strip to each long side of the unit from Step 3. Press. Trim the section to 4½" x 16½".

SECTION E1: HALF-SQUARE TRIANGLES

Finished size: 4" x 28"

Cutting

From black fabric

Cut 2 strips 2⅞" x 40"; crosscut into 14 squares 2⅞" x 2⅞". Stop after every few to square up the edges, as needed. Cut each square in half on the diagonal to make 2 half-square triangles (28 total).

From orange fabric

Cut 2 strips 2⅞" x 40"; crosscut into 14 squares 2⅞" x 2⅞". Stop after every few to square up the edges, as needed. Cut each square in half on the diagonal to make 2 half-square triangles (28 total).

Assembly

1. With right sides together, sew 1 black triangle and 1 orange triangle together along the long bias edge. Press. Make 28.

Make 28.

2. Arrange the units from Step 1 in 2 rows of 14 units each. Sew the units into rows. Press. Sew the rows together. Press.

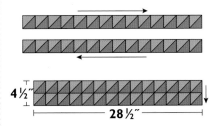

SECTION E2: STITCHING ON PAPER

Finished size: 4" x 28"

Cutting

From assorted orange and black fabrics

Cut 24 strips (approximately) 6" long in widths varying from 1¾" to 3".

Assembly

1. Cut a 4" x 28" piece of paper to use as a foundation.

2. Determine an order for sewing your strips. Place the first strip right side up on one short end of the paper foundation. The top and bottom edges of the strip will overlap the foundation slightly. Stitch down the left edge of the strip with a ⅛"–3/16" seam allowance.

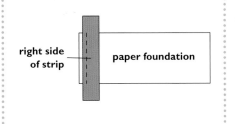

3. Place the second strip over the first strip, with right sides together and the long raw edges even. Pin and sew using a scant ¼" seam allowance. Open the second strip, and press.

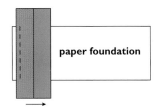

4. Sew the third strip in the same fashion, but this time angle the strip slightly. Be sure that the stitching line includes at least ¼" of fabric on both sides for the entire length. Trim the seam allowance to ¼".

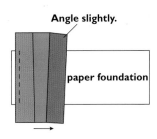

5. Continue adding strips until the paper foundation is completely covered. Angle the strips slightly, and change the direction of the angle every 2 or 3 strips. Trim the section to 4½" x 28½". Remove the paper foundation.

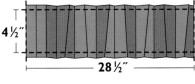

GET CREATIVE!

For added texture and visual interest, insert the cutaway zigzag edges from the Seminole band between two fabric strips. Beads add texture, too.

QUILT ASSEMBLY

1. Refer to Making the Century of Progress Block (pages 14–15) and the block diagram on page 45. Use the A–E sections to construct one 32" block.

2. Refer to Adding Borders (pages 68-69). Measure, trim, and sew a 1¼"-wide inner border strip to the top, bottom, and sides of the quilt. Press the seams toward the border.

3. Fold each inset strip in half lengthwise, wrong sides together. Press. Sew one inset strip and one 3¾"-wide outer border strip together to make a border unit. Make 4.

4. Refer to Borders With Corner Squares (page 69). Measure the quilt through the center from side to side and from top to bottom, including the inner borders you've just added. (The measurements should be the same). Trim the border units from Step 3 to this measurement.

5. Refer to the quilt photo on page 43. Sew a border unit to the top and bottom of the quilt, sandwiching the inset strip between the outer border and the quilt top and aligning the raw edges. Press the seams away from the border unit.

6. Sew a 3¾" corner square to the ends of the remaining border units. Press the seams toward the border units. Sew to the sides of the quilt. Be sure to sandwich the inset strip between the outer border and the quilt top, aligning the raw edges. Press.

FINISHING

1. Refer to Preparing Your Quilt for Quilting (page 69). Layer the quilt top, batting, and backing; baste.

2. Hand or machine quilt as desired. Trim the batting and backing.

3. Use the 3"-wide strips to bind the quilt edges.

4. Add a hanging sleeve and label, if desired.

Small circle; Cut 3.

Large circle; Cut 3.

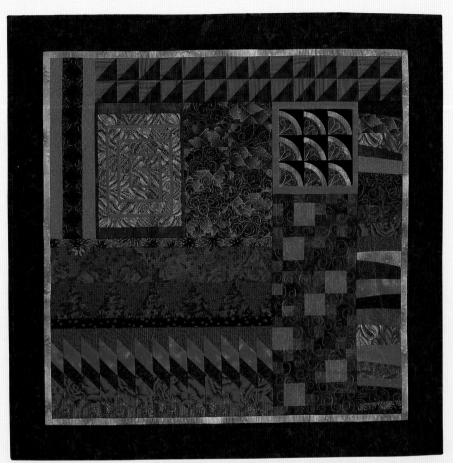

Group Expression—Analogous, 38" x 38", blocks pieced by the group. Setting designed and assembled by M'Liss Rae Hawley. Machine quilted by Barbara Dau, 2003.

A Squeeze of Lime, 36" x 36", pieced and machine quilted by Barbara Dau, 2004.

Mai Tai, 46" x 46", pieced by Susie Kincy. Machine quilted by Barbara Dau, 2004.

Telling Your Story Through Theme: Piecing and Beyond

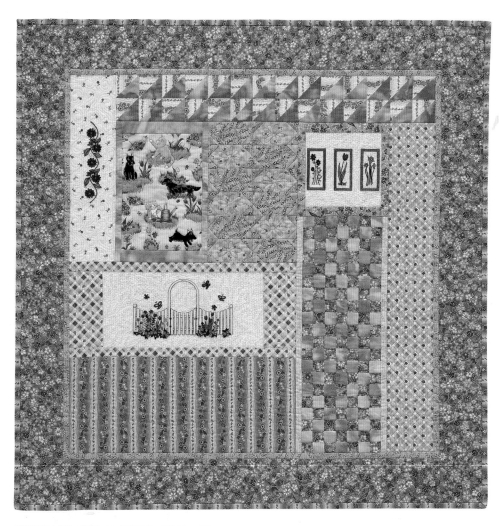

SPRING VIEW FOR ADRIENNE, *45½" x 45½"*,
pieced and machine quilted by M'Liss Rae Hawley, 2004.

This lesson takes the concept of personal expression through color and design even one step further. Rather than focusing on just one or two elements, such as a specific color story or set of piecing techniques, this time you'll combine as many elements as possible—color, theme fabric, piecing, and embellishment (including machine embroidery)—to tell your story.

THE QUILT

Finished quilt size: 45½" x 45½"

Finished block size: 32"

Number of blocks: 1

As in the previous chapter, the quilt for this lesson is made from a single 32" (finished) Century of Progress block. Since the block is so large, the individual sections are also nice and large, giving you lots of room to stretch creatively.

Choose a theme, event, or other inspiration for your quilt's design. Next, select an appropriate color story and piecing and embellishing techniques to express it. I chose springtime as the theme for my quilt *Spring View for Adrienne* (page 54) and expressed my theme primarily through my selection of colors, fabrics, and embroidery motifs, which—in this case—were designed by me to go together. (See Resources on page 79 for embroidery collections.) Then I introduced a few piecing techniques to add richness and visual texture to the overall design.

The block diagram (right) gives you the unfinished size of each section of the block, along with information about where I introduced additional piecing or embellishment. You may duplicate my arrangement or design your own combination of fabric, piecing, and embellishment. Just be

sure the unfinished measurements of the various sections match the measurements shown in the diagram.

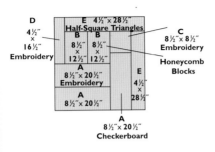

Block diagram—Measurements are for 32" finished block and include ¼" seam allowances.

If you study the photo on page 54, you'll notice that some of the embroidered sections are sized to completely fill the space. Others—such as the one detailed below—are smaller and then enlarged with fabric strips to match the required size. Besides serving a "technical" purpose, the fabric frame adds an extra design element. I did the same with one of the large unpieced (B) sections of the block.

Refer to Quiltmaking Basics (pages 67–73) as needed for guidance with general quiltmaking techniques.

GET CREATIVE!

Here's a way to get your creative juices flowing. Once you've chosen a theme, list related words and images in your Creativity Notebook. (For my springtime/garden theme, I listed words such as flower, watering can, garden gate, tree, pet, bugs, water, and so on.) List as many as you can think of. If you like, add photos, sketches, or other visual images that suggest your theme.

Next, make note of different types of embellishment that might enhance your theme. For example, look for an embroidery collection with related designs, and note how you might customize the thread colors to work with your color story. Do a practice stitch-out, and keep it in your Creativity Notebook for reference. Note (and document) as many embellishment options as occur to you.

I added a fabric frame to this machine-embroidered block.

MATERIAL

Yardages are based on fabric that measures 40" wide after laundering.

1/3 yard each of 12–15 different fabrics in your colors or theme or both for the block

1/4 yard for inner border

1 1/8 yards for outer border

1/2 yard for binding

3 yards for backing

53" x 53" piece of batting

CUTTING THE BORDERS AND BINDING

Cut all strips across the fabric width (selvage to selvage).

From inner border fabric
Cut 4 strips 1" x 40".

From outer border fabric
Cut 5 strips 6 1/2" x 40".

From binding fabric
Cut 6 strips 3" x 40".

QUILT ASSEMBLY

1. Refer to page 45 to cut and construct one 8 1/2" x 20 1/2" Checkerboard section (A), page 49 to cut and construct one 8 1/2" x 12 1/2" Honeycomb Block section (B), and page 51 to cut and construct one 4 1/2" x 28 1/2" Half-Square Triangle section (E). Use the various fabrics in your colors and/or theme.

2. Machine embroider 1 A (8 1/2" x 20 1/2"), 1 C (8 1/2" x 8 1/2"), and 1 D (4 1/2" x 16 1/2"). Use the various fabrics in your colors and/or theme.

> **THINK ABOUT** *making the embroidery into an appliqué for more flexibility in placing the motif.*

3. Refer to the diagram on page 55 to cut any remaining pieces or sections. Use the various fabrics in your colors and/or theme.

4. Refer to Making the Century of Progress Block (pages 14–15) to construct one 32" Century of Progress block. Use pieces A–E or sections that you cut, pieced, or embroidered from your chosen fabrics.

5. Refer to Adding Borders (pages 68-69). Measure, trim, and sew a 1"-wide inner border strip to the top, bottom, and sides of the quilt. Press the seams toward the border.

6. Repeat Step 5 to measure, trim, and sew a 6 1/2"-wide outer border strip to the top, bottom, and sides of the quilt, piecing them as necessary; press.

FINISHING

1. Refer to Preparing Your Quilt for Quilting (page 69). Layer the quilt top, batting, and backing; baste.

2. Hand or machine quilt as desired. Trim the batting and backing.

3. Use the 3"-wide strips to bind the quilt edges.

4. Add a hanging sleeve and label, if desired.

> **ADORN YOUR QUILT** *with ribbon, beads, and buttons. Success is in the details!*

Ready for a Halloween Party, 42" x 42", pieced by Annette Barca. Machine quilted by Barbara Dau, 2004.

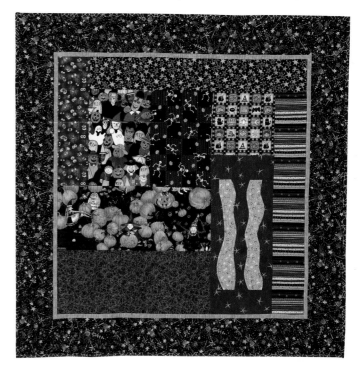

Funky Fowl, *42" x 42", pieced and machine quilted by Bev Green, 2003. Inspired by a Mary Lou Weidman design.*

My Flag, My Country, *31½" x 31½", pieced and machine quilted by Peggy Johnson, 2004.*

Imari, *37" x 37",*
pieced, embellished, and hand
quilted by Vicki DeGraaf, 2004.

To Russia With Love, 46" x 46",
pieced by Anastasia Riordan.
Machine quilted by Barbara
Dau, 2004.

Telling Your Story Through Fabric: Large-Scale Prints

WITH LOVE—SERGEANT A.W. HAWLEY 2/7 ECHO CO., 46½" x 62½", *pieced by M'Liss Rae Hawley. Machine quilted by Barbara Dau, 2004.*

Here's a chance to really have fun with fabric! In this lesson, you'll rely on the motif of the fabric as the main tool to tell your story. Theme-related, large-scale prints take center stage, and an enlarged, elongated block provides a nicely scaled canvas to show them off. You can use appliqués, as I did (large hearts, flags, and emblems), to camouflage awkward or partial motifs that result from cutting these large prints.

Be sure to add a supporting cast of smaller-scale prints to the larger scale ones for visual balance.

THE QUILT

Finished quilt size: 46½" x 62½"

Finished block size: 32" x 48"

Number of blocks: 1

The quilt for this lesson is a single Century of Progress block, enlarged and stretched to 32" x 48"—or a 4:6 ratio (see page 29). Once you've chosen a theme, begin your hunt for large-scale, theme-related prints to support it. Do you typically collect this type of fabric? Go to your fabric collection, and have a look. See where your existing stash takes you: one, two, possibly three theme-related fabrics?

Next, take your hunt to the fabric store. One shop may not have enough variety, so visit another (and another!) if you can. Look through mail-order catalogs or shop online. Large-scale prints are worth the treasure hunt—your fun (and possibly funky) quilt will be the reward!

GET CREATIVE!

You may prefer to do this lesson in reverse. Instead of choosing the fabrics to match your theme, amass a collection of related large-scale print fabrics, and let them dictate the theme for your quilt. Use your Creativity Notebook to catalog your swatches, and carry it with you when you shop to build your collection.

Because I was making this quilt for my son, Alexander, a Marine serving overseas, I chose fabrics with a patriotic theme. Rather than focusing on the typical stars-and-stripes, I refined my theme even further and searched for patriotic prints with a nostalgic, 1940s pinup girl flavor. Smaller-scaled, more traditional prints were added for balance.

If you study my quilt, you'll see that I occasionally incorporated a narrow strip of fabric into one of the larger pieces in my quilt. These strips provide a visual "break"—in color, value, or scale—between the many large-scale prints and keep them from "mushing" together. You may decide to incorporate these visual breaks as well, placing them as dictated by the fabrics in your quilt. Just be sure the unfinished measurements of the overall piece match the measurements shown in the block diagram (page 29).

I incorporated a contrasting strip of blue fabric as a visual break between two large-scale prints.

Refer to Quiltmaking Basics (pages 67-73) as needed for guidance with general quiltmaking techniques.

> *A quilt is a wonderful analogy for life—*
>
> *Multilayered and as colorful as you permit.*
>
> *Let your personality and your personal history guide you in a colorful and exciting quilt adventure!*

MATERIAL

Yardages are based on fabric that measures 40" wide after laundering.

⅜ yard of 12 different fabrics in your colors and theme for block

¼ yard for corner squares

¼ yard for inner border

1⅛ yards for outer border

⅔ yard for binding

2⅝ yards for backing

54½" x 70½" piece of batting

CUTTING

Cut all strips across the fabric width (selvage to selvage).

From the assorted fabrics in your chosen theme and colors

Cut 1 piece 8½" x 30½" (A1).

Cut 2 pieces 12½" x 20½" (A2).

Cut 2 pieces 8½" x 18½" (B).

Cut 1 piece 8½" x 12½" (C).

Cut 1 piece 4½" x 24½" (D).

Cut 1 piece 6½" x 28½" (E1).

Cut 1 piece 4½" x 42½" (E2).
(Piece together 2 strips, if necessary.)

From corner square fabric
Cut 4 squares 6½" x 6½".

From inner border fabric
Cut 5 strips 1½" x 40".

From outer border fabric
Cut 5 strips 6½" x 40".

From binding fabric
Cut 7 strips 3" x 40".

QUILT ASSEMBLY

1. Refer to Making the Century of Progress Block (pages 14–15) and the block diagram on page 29 to construct one 32" x 48" Century of Progress block. Use pieces A–E that you cut from your chosen fabrics.

2. Refer to Adding Borders (pages 68-69). Measure, trim, and sew a 1½"-wide border strip to the top, bottom, and sides of the quilt, piecing them as necessary. Press the seams toward the border.

3. Refer to Borders With Corner Squares (page 69). Measure the quilt through the center from side to side and from top to bottom, including the borders you've just added.

Trim two 6½"-wide border strips to each measurement, piecing them as necessary. Sew the shorter border strips to the top and bottom of the quilt. Press the seams toward the border.

4. Sew a 6½" corner square to the ends of the remaining border units. Press the seams toward the border units. Sew to the sides of the quilt. Press.

FINISHING

1. Refer to Preparing Your Quilt for Quilting (page 69). Layer the quilt top, batting, and backing; baste.

2. Hand or machine quilt as desired. Trim the backing and batting.

3. Use the 3"-wide strips to bind the quilt edges.

4. Add a hanging sleeve and label, if desired.

Refreshing All Year Long, 46" x 61", pieced by M'Liss Rae Hawley. Machine quilted by Barbara Dau, 2002.

Chickens in My Backyard, 46" x 62",
*pieced by Peggy J. Johnson. Machine
quilted by Barbara Dau, 2004.*

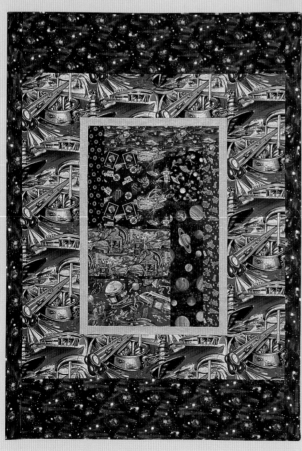

Jason's Fantasy World, 71" x 100",
*pieced by Susie Kincy. Machine quilted by
Barbara Dau, 2004.*

Telling Your Story With Friends: Group Quilts

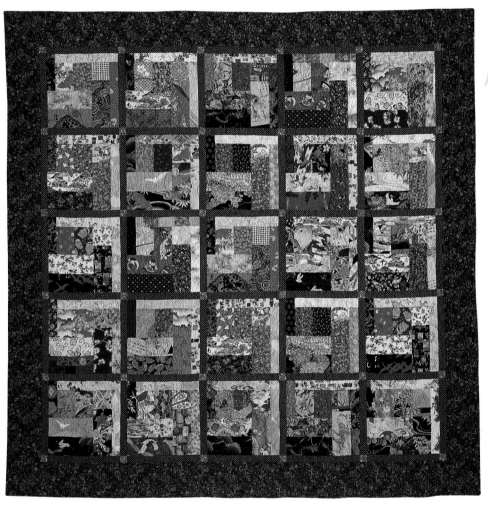

CENTURY OF PROGRESS FOR MICHAEL, *100" x 97". Blocks made by the group.*
Setting designed and pieced by M'Liss Rae Hawley. Machine quilted by Doris Ellis, 2003.

This lesson is an exercise in group creativity—and one that you might like to try with your best quilting buddies.

As we reached the end of our study of color and design, I presented my group of quilters with a unique assignment. I instructed each to select a color story or theme or both and "challenge" the others to make a Century of Progress block to fit the specific criteria.

The challenge was a huge success on many levels. As each quilter made the blocks for the others in the group, she was stretched to try different color stories, often involving combinations she would never have considered on her own. When the others returned the blocks she specified, she faced the challenge of designing a quilt to showcase them.

As you can see from the quilts in this chapter, the results were amazing, embracing a wide variety of color stories, themes, settings, and sizes!

Tide Pools, 64" x 79". Blocks made by the group. Setting designed and pieced by Peggy J. Johnson. Machine quilted by Barbara Dau, 2004.

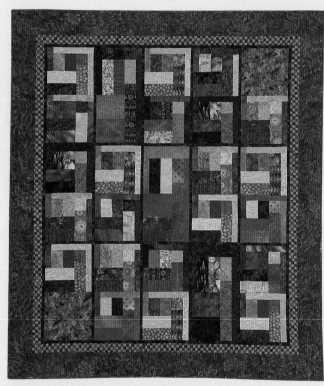

From the Warm Side, 53" x 60". Blocks made by the group. Setting designed, pieced, and machine quilted by Barbara Dau, 2004.

Windows to Africa, 65" x 65". Blocks made by the group. Setting designed and pieced by Anastasia Riordan. Machine quilted by Barbara Dau, 2004.

Summer Meadow Land, *58" x 73½". Blocks made by the group. Setting designed and pieced by Vicki DeGraaf. Machine quilted by Barbara Dau, 2004.*

Element of Beauty, *73" x 73". Blocks made by the group. Setting designed, pieced, and machine quilted by Stacie Johnson, 2004.*

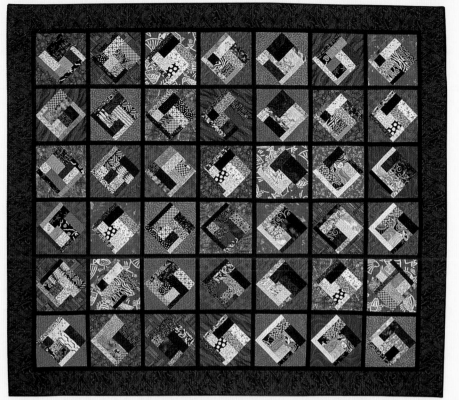

A Case in Point, *98" x 86". Blocks made by the group. Setting designed and pieced by Larkin Van Horn. Machine quilted by Barbara Dau, 2004.*

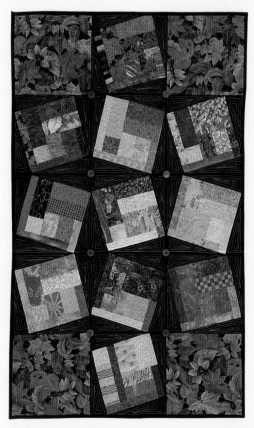

Wonky Blocks, *29½" x 49". Blocks made by the group. Setting designed, pieced, and machine quilted by Larkin Van Horn, 2004.*

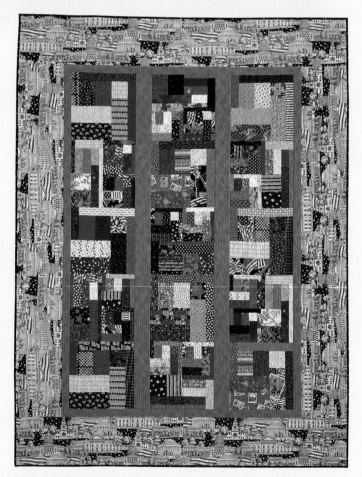

Michael's Red, White, and Blue, *86" x 106". Blocks made by the group. Setting designed and pieced by Susie Kincy. Machine quilted by Barbara Dau, 2004.*

Quiltmaking Basics

SQUARING FABRIC FOR ROTARY CUTTING

Almost all the pieces for the blocks and quilts in this book can be cut with a rotary cutter. It is essential that you square the edges of your fabrics before you rotary cut them into strips and pieces. The edges of the fabric must be straight for the resulting pieces to be straight, and you don't want to waste time—or precious fabric!—by having to stop and recut. Make sure the fabric is pressed and that you fold it carefully before you begin cutting.

Note: Cutting instructions are for right-handers. Reverse if you are left-handed.

1. Fold the fabric from selvage to selvage (or from selvage to cut edge for a fat quarter).

2. Hold the fabric in the air, and study the drape. Disregard the cut ends; instead move the selvages from side to side until the fabric is perfectly flat.

3. Place the fabric on your cutting mat, and make a second fold, selvage edge to folded edge. If you have a large piece of fabric, try to break it down so you can work with a more manageable amount.

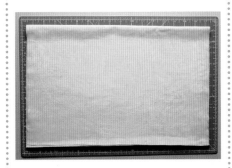

If you are squaring up a fat quarter, you just need to make the first fold from selvage to cut edge. If there is no selvage to guide you, make the fold lengthwise grain to lengthwise grain. You can easily tell the lengthwise grain: it's the edge of the fabric that has no stretch.

To Square up your Fabric

1. Place the folded fabric on the cutting mat with the folded edge facing you. Position your ruler on the right edge of the fabric so it is perpendicular to the fold.

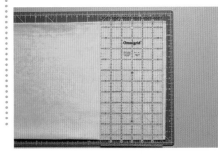

2. Trim a narrow strip from the edge of the fabric to square it up. Rotate the fabric (or the mat), and repeat to trim the opposite edge.

CUTTING STRIPS AND PIECES

Use your ruler, not the markings on the mat, to measure and cut strips and pieces. I use the grid on my mat to align the fabric and for taking general measurements, not for making precise measurements.

Working with the squared left edge of the fabric, use your ruler to measure and cut a strip of the desired width. Repeat to cut the required number of strips. You may want to square up the edge of the fabric after every few cuts.

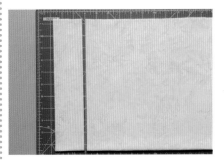

Cut the strip into squares or other smaller segments as directed in the project instructions.

PIECING AND PRESSING

Unless otherwise noted, you'll be using a ¼" seam allowance for piecing the blocks and quilts in this book. It's always a good idea to stitch a test piece to check that your ¼" seam is accurate before beginning to sew.

The construction process is simple: you'll sew pieces into units, units into rows or sections, and the rows or sections together to complete the block or the quilt. The block and project instructions will tell you which way to press the seams, either in the step itself or with arrows in the accompanying diagrams.

Press lightly in a lifting-and-lowering motion. Dragging the iron across the fabric can distort the individual pieces and finished blocks.

ASSEMBLING THE QUILT

The quilts in this book are sewn together in two basic arrangements or sets: the straight set and the diagonal set.

In a straight set, the blocks are arranged in horizontal rows, with the block edges parallel to the sides of the quilt. The blocks are sewn together with ¼" seams to create the rows, with seams pressed in opposite directions from row to row. The rows are sewn together, and seams pressed, usually in one direction.

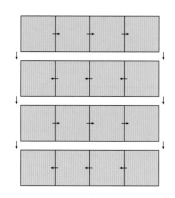

Straight set—Arrows indicate pressing direction.

In a diagonal set, the blocks are turned "on point," with their edges at a 45° angle to the sides of the quilt. The blocks are arranged in diagonal rows, and the zigzag edges are filled in with half- and quarter-square triangles to "straighten" the quilt top. (The project instructions tell you how many of these triangles to cut and how big to cut them.) The blocks and side triangles are sewn together with ¼" seams to create the diagonal rows, with seams pressed in opposite directions from row to row. The corner triangles are added next, and finally the rows are sewn together and pressed.

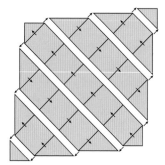

Diagonal set—Arrows indicate pressing direction.

ADDING BORDERS

The quilts in this book feature two different border treatments: squared borders and borders with corner squares.

Squared Borders

Squared borders are the easiest of all borders to sew. Add the top and bottom borders first and then the side borders.

1. Measure the quilt top through the center from side to side, and cut 2 border strips to this measurement. These will be the top and bottom borders.

2. Place pins at the center point of the top and bottom of the quilt top, as well as at the center point of each border strip. Pin the borders to the quilt top, matching the ends and center points. Use additional pins as needed, easing or gently stretching the border to fit.

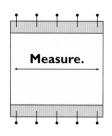

Pin border strips to top and bottom.

3. Sew the borders to the quilt with a ¼" seam. Press as instructed—usually toward the border. If the quilt top is slightly longer than the border, stitch with the quilt top on the bottom, closest to the feed dogs. If the reverse is true, stitch with the border on the bottom. The motion of the feed dogs will help ease in the extra length.

4. Measure the quilt top from top to bottom, including the borders you've just sewn, and cut 2 border strips to this measurement. These will be the side borders. Repeat Steps 2 and 3 to pin, sew, and press the borders.

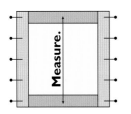

Pin border strips to sides.

Borders With Corner Squares

Instructions for *In Transition* (page 43) and *With Love—Sergeant A.W. Hawley 2/7 Echo Co.* (page 59) include borders with corner squares. Some of the quilts made by members of the group include corner squares as well.

1. Measure the quilt through the center from side to side and from top to bottom. Cut 2 border strips to each of these measurements.

2. Sew the appropriately sized strips to the top and bottom of the quilt. Press the seams toward the border. Sew the corner squares to each end of the 2 remaining border strips. Press the seams toward the border strip. Sew the strips to the sides of the quilt; press.

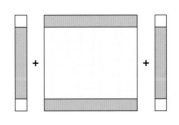

Borders with corner squares

Preparing Your Quilt for Quilting

As with every step of quiltmaking, this step is important. Don't skimp here! Take time to layer properly and baste sufficiently. The results—a nice, flat quilt, free from puckers and bumps—will make you proud.

Batting

Choice of batting is a personal decision, but you'll want to consider the method (and amount) of quilting you plan to do, as well as the quilt's end use. Since I prefer machine quilting (see pages 70-71), I usually use cotton batting in a heavier weight for bed quilts and wallhangings and a lighter weight for clothing. You'll probably want to stick with lightweight batting for hand quilting. Polyester batting is a good choice for tied quilts.

No matter which type of batting you choose, cut the batting approximately 4" larger than the quilt top on all sides.

Backing

As with the batting, you'll want the quilt backing to be approximately 4" larger than the quilt top on all sides. You'll sometimes need to piece the

fabric to have a large enough backing piece. Prewash the backing fabric and remove the selvages first.

Layering and Basting

Unlike many machine quilters, I prefer to hand baste with thread rather than to pin baste. That allows me to machine quilt without having to stop to remove pins.

1. Carefully press the quilt top from the back to set the seams, and then press from the front. Press the backing. If you wish, use spray starch or sizing.

2. Spread the backing wrong side up on a clean, flat surface, and secure it with masking tape. The fabric should be taut, but not stretched. Center the batting over the backing, and secure. Finally, center the quilt top over the batting.

3. Thread a long needle with light-colored thread. Beginning in the center of the quilt, stitch a 4" grid of horizontal and vertical lines.

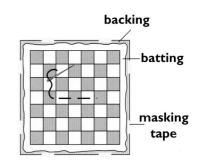

4. When you've finished basting, remove the tape and get ready to quilt!

QUILTING

A quilt becomes a quilt when it includes three layers—a top, a filler layer or batting, and a backing—all attached with stitching of some type to hold the layers together. (That means, to call your project a quilt, you need to finish it!) Some quilters create that stitching by hand, others by machine. My quilts in this book—as well as almost all the quilts made by my wonderful group of quilters—are machine quilted.

Machine Quilting

Each step of the quiltmaking process is exciting and fun to me, including the machine quilting. I love the idea of adding yet another level of creativity to my quilts. Machine quilting my own tops gives me flexibility in making those design decisions, and I do my own quilting whenever I can. Because of time constraints, however, I find I must now have many of my quilt tops professionally machine quilted. If you have stacks of quilt tops waiting to be quilted, you might want to consider that option, too.

Machine quilting is an art form, so there is a learning curve involved. Practice is the best way to learn and master this skill. Here are some guidelines to get you started.

Dual-Feed Foot

The dual-feed foot (page 12) is designed to hold and feed the three layers of your quilt evenly as you stitch. Use this foot to stitch single or parallel lines and grids—whether vertical, horizontal, or diagonal. You can also use this foot when you use certain decorative stitches and embellishing techniques, such as couching (page 75), to machine quilt.

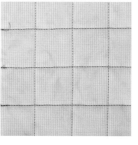

Use a dual-feed foot for straight-line quilting.

My favorite decorative stitch is the serpentine stitch, which I use for machine quilting, for couching decorative threads, and for finishing the edges of my quilts before I add the binding (see pages 71-73). A very versatile stitch, it takes on a totally different appearance with just a change in its width and length.

Serpentine stitch

Open-Toe Stippling Foot

Also called a darning foot, the open-toe stippling foot (shown on page 12) allows you to quilt in all directions: you are the guide! Use this foot for stipple quilting, meandering, and other free-motion techniques.

Use an open-toe foot for free-motion quilting.

You will need to drop the feed dogs on your sewing machine when you use the open-toe stippling foot. You may also need to set the presser foot pressure to the darning position so you can move the quilt at a smooth pace for consistent stitches. Some machines have a built-in stipple stitch, which is a wonderful way to achieve this beautiful surface texture.

I like to stipple quilt around machine-embroidered motifs. This causes the embroidered design to "pop out" and become a focal point.

I combined stipple quilting with machine embroidery in Spring View for Adrienne. For a full view of this quilt, see page 54.

Threads

I consider quilting thread to be a design element, not just the means to hold the three layers of my quilt together. I also believe that variety in thread adds visual interest and showcases the individuality of the quilter. For these reasons, I frequently use a mix of threads in my quilts. When choosing thread, I consider thread color, texture, and weight and where I plan to use the thread.

Typical thread choices for machine quilting include rayon (35- and 40-weight), cotton, polyester, and monofilament. I use lots of variegated and metallic threads and novelty threads, such as Twister Tweeds, Swirling Sensation, and Moon Glow. The latter are manufactured by Robison-Anton. (See Resources, page 79.)

Some of my favorite threads for machine quilting

Design

Let your imagination be your guide in choosing quilting motifs for your quilts. Design sources are everywhere! Look carefully at quilts in museums, shows, books, and magazines; at books of quilting patterns; and at quilting stencils. Observe patterns in other areas of your life—particularly patterns in nature.

In addition to the basics (in-the-ditch, outline, straight-line, and stipple quilting), try filling in open spaces with loops, curves, clamshells, and waves. Combine straight and curvy lines for variety.

Another option is to let the fabric inspire you and to simply follow a pattern in the fabric with your stitching. Create a garden trellis over a floral fabric, or add detail to a beach with quilted rocks and shells.

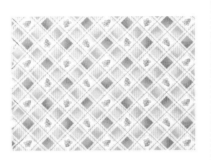
Fabric motifs are great inspiration for quilting designs.

FINISHING YOUR QUILT

Your quilt's bindings, hanging sleeve, and label are important too, so be sure to give them the same attention you've given to every other step of the process.

Squaring Up

Before adding the binding, you need to trim the excess batting and backing and square up your quilt. Use the seam of the outer border as a guide.

1. Align a ruler with the outer border seam and measure to the edge of the quilt in a number of places. Use the narrowest measurement as a guide for positioning your ruler, and trim the excess batting and backing all around the quilt.

2. Fold the quilt in half lengthwise and crosswise to check that the corners are square and the sides are equal in length. If not, use a large square ruler to correct this, one corner at a time.

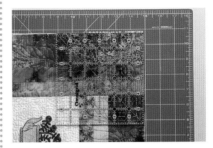
Square up the corners.

3. Stabilize the edges of the quilt by stitching around the perimeter with a basting or serpentine stitch. (Do not use a zigzag stitch.)

Serpentine stitch around quilt perimeter

4. Remove any stray threads or bits of batting from the quilt top, and you are ready to bind your quilt.

Making and Applying Binding

Binding is an important and, sadly, often overlooked step in the quilt-making process. Many a wonderful quilt is spoiled by a poorly sewn binding. Take your time deciding what fabric you will use, and enjoy the process of stitching it to your quilt. You're coming down the home stretch now!

Typically, I cut binding strips 3" wide from selvage to selvage across the width of the fabric. I make an exception and cut strips on the bias only when I want to create a special effect with a plaid or striped fabric or when I need to follow a curved or rounded edge.

The following method is the one I use to bind my quilts. It results in a finished edge that is attractive and strong.

1. Cut enough binding strips to go around the perimeter (outside edges) of the quilt plus an extra 10" for seams and corners. Sew the strips together at right angles, as shown. Trim the excess fabric, leaving a ¼" seam allowance, and press the seams open.

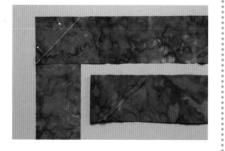

2. Fold the binding in half lengthwise, wrong sides together, and press.

3. Starting 6" from the upper left corner and with the raw edges even, lay the binding on the quilt top. Check to see that none of the mitered seams falls on a corner of

the quilt. If so, adjust the starting point. Begin stitching 4" from the end of the binding, using a ½" seam allowance.

4. Stitch about 2", stop, and cut the threads. Remove the quilt from the machine, and fold the binding to the back of the quilt. The binding should cover the line of machine stitching on the back. If the binding overlaps the stitching too much, try again, stitching just outside the first line of stitching. If the binding doesn't cover the original line of stitching, stitch just inside the line. Remove the unwanted stitches before you continue.

5. Using the position you determined for stitching in Step 4, resume stitching until you are ½" from the first corner of the quilt. Stop, cut the thread, and remove the quilt from the machine.

6. Fold the binding to create a mitered corner. Resume stitching, mitering each corner as you come to it.

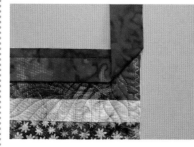

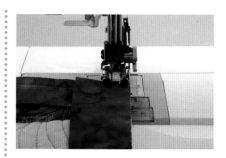

7. Stop stitching about 3" after you've turned the last corner. Make sure the starting and finishing ends of the binding overlap by at least 4". Cut the threads, and remove the quilt from the machine. Measure a 3" overlap, and trim the excess binding.

8. Lay the quilt right side up. Unfold the unstitched tails, place them right sides together at right angles, and pin. Draw a line from the upper left corner to the lower right corner of the binding, as shown, and stitch on the drawn line.

9. Carefully trim the seam allowance to ¼", and press the seam open. Refold the binding and press. Finish stitching the binding to the quilt.

10. Turn the binding to the back of the quilt, and pin. (I pin approximately 12" at a time.) Using matching-colored thread, blindstitch the binding to the quilt back, carefully mitering the corners as you approach them. Hand stitch the miters on both sides.

Making and Adding a Sleeve

If you want to display your quilt on a wall, you need to add a sleeve to protect your work of art from undue strain.

1. Cut an 8½"-wide strip of backing fabric 1" shorter than the width of the quilt. (If the quilt is wider than 40", cut 2 strips and stitch them together, end to end.) Fold the short ends under ¼", stitch, and press.

2. Fold the sleeve lengthwise, right sides together. Sew the long raw edges, and press. Turn the sleeve right side out, and press again.

3. Match the center point of the top edge of the quilt with the center point of the sleeve. Pin the sleeve to the quilt, right below the binding. Use matching-colored thread to blindstitch the top edge in place.

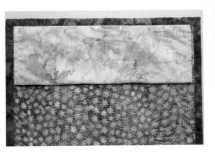

4. Push the bottom edge of the sleeve up a tiny bit so that when inserted, the hanging rod does not put strain on the quilt. Blindstitch the bottom edge of the sleeve, taking care not to catch the front of the quilt as you stitch.

Creating a Label

I always recommend that you make a label for your quilt. This gives you a place to provide important information about both you and your quilt. I like to make my labels large—about 4" x 7"—so I have plenty of room. You can sew the label to the lower right corner of the quilt back before it is quilted, or wait until after the quilt is complete.

I suggest you always include the following information on your label: the name of the quilt; your full name (and business name, if you have one); your city, county, province and/or state, and country of residence; and the date.

If the quilt was made for a special person, to commemorate a special event, or as part of a series, you may want to include that information as well. You may also choose to note the name of the quilting teacher who inspired you, or tell a special story connected to the quilt.

You can make a simple label by drawing and writing on fabric with permanent fabric markers. (Stabilize the fabric first with freezer paper or interfacing.) For a more elaborate (and fun!) label, try photo-transfer techniques, use the lettering system on your sewing machine, or use an embroidery machine to embellish your label. You may even want to create your own distinctive signature or logo. Include patches, decals, buttons, ribbons, or lace. I often include leftover blocks to tie the quilt top to the back.

Use the label to record key information about your quilt.

Embellishment

As you progress in the creative journey of quiltmaking, you will eventually discover embellishment—the wonderful process of decorating your quilt with threads, trims, beads, buttons, and other ornamentation. This ornamentation enhances the quilt, reinforcing the color story and the theme.

Begin, as always, by reducing your variables. When considering potential threads, trims, buttons, and beads for your quilt, keep in mind the parameters you have set forth in regard to the quilt's theme, color story, scale, and size. Once you've zeroed in on the specifics, the more embellishment options you have to choose from, the better. Surround yourself with as many choices as possible; the beautiful ornaments will inspire you to be more creative. Place the various embellishments beside or on top of your quilt-in-progress: look at them, play with them, think about them. Don't worry about what you don't end up using. The ribbons and trims left over from this quilt will become inspiration for the next.

As you design and execute your plan for embellishment, remember the "power of one." I planned for all five of my dachshunds to be represented on *Follow the Path— The Journey Continues* (page 37). As it turned out, one dog had far more impact. I'll spotlight the other four in different media on another project—or projects.

Embellishment is all about detail. Pay attention. Take time to observe the direction your quilt is going. This is also an opportunity to take risks: to use threads and

other products that are new to you, to attempt new techniques, and to combine colors and textures in innovative ways. Most important, be creative and have fun with embellishment!

The following are just some of the many items you can use for embellishment.

Novelty threads and trims, cording, ribbons, rickrack, and tassels

Beads, sequins, buttons, and costume jewelry

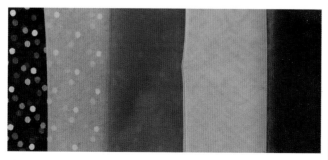

Colored, glittered, and patterned tulle

Decorator fabrics and novelty fabrics such as metallics and Mylar

Once you've gathered a selection of embellishing materials, here are some techniques you can try.

Collage

Couching

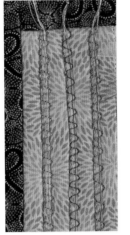

Decorative machine stitching

Machine embroidery stitched on the fabric or used to create an appliqué

Free-motion embroidery

Beading

Raw-edge, fusible, and three-dimensional appliqué

FOLLOW THE PATH— THE JOURNEY CONTINUES: AN EMBELLISHMENT STORY

As you've worked through the various lessons in this book, you've already discovered that reducing your variables to a single color story is a great place to start in designing a quilt. The assignment for The Analogous Color Story (pages 37–40) is to create a triptych—or three-paneled quilt—in an analogous color scheme. This three-panel format is ideal not only for exploring a new color story, but also for experimenting with embellishment. The following describes the process I used to choose and add embellishment to my triptych *Follow the Path—The Journey Continues* (page 37). This quilt was a personal journey for me in many ways. I hope my embellishment "story" helps you with your creative and technical journey.

Guided by the assignment, I selected the analogous color story of green, yellow-green, and yellow, and I limited my choice of embellishment—as well as fabric—to that palette.

Fabrics, threads, and other embellishments I considered for Follow the Path—The Journey Continues

The next decision was to choose a theme or story for my quilt, which I did fairly easily.

I determined that the embellishment would include machine embroidery with motifs from my embroidery collections (see page 79). I gathered the rest of the decoration in several shopping trips.

The first step was to select the embroidery motifs and to embroider the panels. I put all my green, yellow-green, and yellow rayon thread next to the embroidery module. I used a different combination of colored thread in each bunch of tiger lilies. I placed other embroidery motifs with the placement of the final "path" in mind. At this point, I also decided which embroideries would be applied later as appliqués. I created these in a hoop with silk organdy and stabilizer.

Detail of the appliquéd embroidery on Follow the Path—The Journey Continues

Next I had to decide how the machine quilting would integrate with the embellishment. I viewed the three panels and each fabric as a separate entity. I created a quilt diagram and filled it in with my machine-quilting design ideas. Because my quilt tells a story, I decided to continue it with my choice of quilting motifs—rain, waterfall, waves, wind, earth, and sky—and with my selection of thread. In addition, I did decorative stitching, outline quilted the various embroideries and motifs in the fabrics, stipple quilted, and quilted curves—both single and overlapping— and grids. I used threads in various weights and in many different tints and shades of my chosen colors.

Detail of the quilting on Follow the Path—The Journey Continues

After I had squared up, bound, and added the sleeve pocket to each panel, it was time to place the embellishment that would signify the "path" in the quilt's title. I started with a layer of glitter tulle. Next I twisted and turned ribbons and attached all to the panels with crystals and beads, also in the analogous colors of my original color story. To finish, I added the primroses and dachshund, which I appliquéd with a free-motion zigzag stitch.

Detail of the tulle, ribbon, and embroidered "path" on Follow the Path—The Journey Continues

Gallery

Is It Halloween?, 59" x 59", pieced by Annette Barca. Machine quilted by Barbara Dau, 2004.

Who Spilled the Crayons?, 25" x 25", pieced and machine quilted by Annette Barca, 2004.

Red Dragonfly Vest (front and back view), by Peggy J. Johnson, 2004.

Purple Eve, *50" x 58", pieced by Anastasia Riordan.*
Machine quilted by Barbara Dau, 2004.

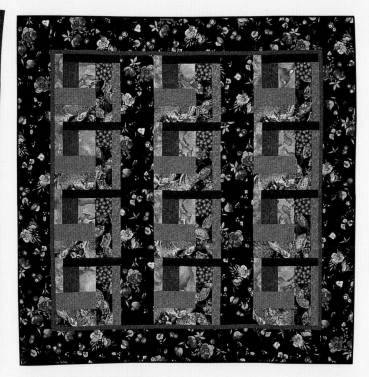

Japanese Medley, *81" x 81",*
pieced by Anastasia Riordan.
Machine quilted by Barbara Dau, 2004.

Africa, My Africa, *75" x 79",*
pieced by Anastasia Riordan.
Machine quilted by Barbara Dau, 2004.

Bibliography

Barnes, Christine, *Color: The Quilters' Guide*, That Patchwork Place: Bothell, WA, 1997

Bothwell, Dorr and Marlys Mayfield, *NOTAN: The Dark-Light Principle of Design*, Dover Publications, Inc.: New York, 1991

Cream, Penelope (senior editor), *The Color Book: 11,264 Color Combinations*, Chronicle Books: San Francisco, CA, 1997

De Grandis, Luigina, *Theory and Use of Color*, Prentice-Hall, Inc.: Englewood Cliffs, NJ, and Harry N. Abrams, Inc.: New York, 1987

Hope, Augustine and Margaret Walch, *Living Colors*, Chronicle Books: San Francisco, CA, 2002

Ipsen, David C., *Isaac Newton, Reluctant Genius*, Enslow Publishers, Inc.: Hillside, NJ, 1985

Itten, Johannes, *The Art of Color: The Subjective Experience and Objective Rationale of Color*, translated by Ernst von Haagen, John Wiley & Sons, Inc.: Hoboken, NJ, 1997

Itten, Johannes, *The Elements of Color*, translated by Ernst von Haagen, John Wiley & Sons, Inc.: Hoboken, NJ, 1997

Kobayashi, Shigenobu, *Color Image Scale*, translated by Louella Matsunaga, Kodansha America, Inc.: Tokyo, 1990

Krochmal, Arnold and Connie Krochmal, *The Complete Illustrated Book of Dyes From Natural Sources*, Doubleday & Company, Inc.: Garden City, NY, 1974

Larsen, Jack Lenor and Jeanne Weeks, *Fabrics for Interiors: A Guide for Architects, Designers, and Consumers*, John Wiley & Sons, Inc.: Hoboken, NJ, 1997

Locher, J.L., F.H. Bool, et al., *M.C. Escher: His Life and Complete Graphic Work*, Abradale Press, Harry N. Abrams, Inc.: New York, 1992

McKelvey, Susan, *The Classic American Quilt Collection: Creative Ideas for Color and Fabric*, Rodale Press, Inc.: Emmaus, PA, 1996

Penders, Mary Coyne, *Color and Cloth*, NTC Publishing Group: San Francisco, CA, 1995

Pizzuto, Joseph J., Arthur Price, Allen C. Cohen, and Ingrid Johnson, *Fabric Science*, Fairchild Books: New York, 1999

Rossbach, Sarah and Lin Yun, *Living Color: Master Lin Yun's Guide to Feng Shui and the Art of Color*, Kodansha America, Inc.: New York, 1994

Schultz, Pearle and Harry Schultz, *Isaac Newton, Scientific Genius*, Garrard Publishing Co.: Champaign, IL, 1972

Silver Dolphin, *Bright Ideas for Your Home*, Thunder Bay Press: San Diego, CA, 1997

Van Horn, Larkin Jean, *Beadwork for Fabric Artists: Larkin's Encyclopaedia of Bead Stitches*, Larkin Van Horn (self-published), 2004

Wilson, Jose and Arthur Leaman, *Color in Decoration: A Guide to the Use of Color in Contemporary and Traditional Interiors*, Van Nostrand Reinhold Co.: New York, and Studio Vista Limited: London, 1979

Wolfrom, Joen, *The Magical Effects of Color*, C&T Publishing: Lafayette, CA, 1992

Resources

For quilting supplies:

Cotton Patch Mail Order
3405 Hall Lane, Dept. CTB
Lafayette, CA 94549
(800) 835-4418
(925) 283-7883
Email: quiltusa@yahoo.com
Website: www.quiltusa.com

In the Beginning
8291 Lake City Way N.E.
Seattle, WA 98115
(206) 523-8862

Note: Fabric manufacturers discontinue fabrics regularly. Exact fabrics shown may no longer be available.

For information about thread:

Robison-Anton Textiles
P.O. Box 159
Fairview, NJ 07022
Website: www.robison-anton.com

Embroidery Collections

These embroidery collections and more are available at your local participating Husqvarna Viking, Pfaff and White dealer.

Follow the Path—The Journey Continues (page 37)
My Favorite Quilt Designs, Disk Part #756 253300, multiformat CD-ROM, and Spring View, Disk Part #756 255100, multiformat CD-ROM, both by M'Liss Rae Hawley

A Little Bit of Sparkle (page 30)
Shimmering Paisleys, Disk Part #556 252300, multiformat CD-ROM

Spring View for Adrienne (page 54)
Roses, Embroidery 17, and Spring View, Disk Part #756 255100, multiformat CD-ROM, by M'Liss Rae Hawley

About the Author

M'Liss Rae Hawley is an accomplished quilting teacher, lecturer, embroidery and textile designer, and best-selling author. She conducts workshops and seminars throughout North America. As the author of five books, including *Phenomenal Fat Quarter Quilts* (2004), and the originator of numerous innovative designs, M'Liss is constantly seeking new boundaries to challenge her students while imparting her enthusiasm and love for the art of quilting.

Although she is in production for her new PBS television series, *M'Liss's Quilting World*, M'Liss continues to create fabric with coordinating embroidery collections, write books, and create patterns for *McCall's Quilting* magazine. She likes to break quilting down to the basics to show students that quilting can be easy and fun at any level of skill!

M'Liss and her husband, Michael, live on Whidbey Island, Washington, in a filbert orchard. Michael is also a best-selling author and the sheriff of Island County. Their son, Alexander, is in the Marine Corps, and their daughter, Adrienne, is in college. Michael and M'Liss share their home with five dachshunds and three cats.

M'liss and her group of quilters. Front row, left to right:
Susie Kincy, M'Liss, Peggy Johnson, Vicki DeGraaf. Back row, left to right: Anastasia
Riordan, Larkin Van Horn, Annette Barca, Barbara Dau, and Stacie Johnson.
Not pictured: Bev Green.

Another C&T book
by M'Liss Rae Hawley